The Self-Reliant Kitchen

The Self-Reliant Kitchen

From-Scratch Sourdough Breads, Homemade Cheese, and Farm-to-Table Meals

Michelle Mullennix

Skyhorse Publishing

Skyhorse Publishing books may be purchased in bulk at special discounts
for sales promotion, corporate gifts, fund-raising, or educational
purposes. Special editions can also be created to specifications. For details,
contact the Special Sales Department, Skyhorse Publishing, 307 West
36th Street, 11th Floor, New York, NY 10018 or info@skyhorsepublishing.com.

Skyhorse® and Skyhorse Publishing® are registered trademarks of
Skyhorse Publishing, Inc.®, a Delaware corporation.

Visit our website at www.skyhorsepublishing.com.

10 9 8 7 6 5 4 3 2

Library of Congress Cataloging-in-Publication Data is available on file.

Cover design by Kai Texel
Cover photos by Michelle Mullennix, Bonnie Matthews, and Hannah Mesic

Print ISBN: 978-1-5107-7811-5
Ebook ISBN: 978-1-5107-7927-3

Printed in China

Table of Contents

Introduction

Welcome to the homestead!

First off, thank you! This book has been a labor of love, one that I have poured my heart into, so your support means more to me and my family than I could ever put into words. Whether you want to be more self-reliant, become better at sourcing your ingredients, learn a few traditional cooking skills, or just want some recipes to create nourishing meals for your family, this is the book for you! Heritage cooking, making things from scratch, farm to table–all of the things that I am so passionate about now–were not things I grew up with. Other than horses, I did not grow up with animals, we didn't grow or raise our own food, and I had no idea how butter was actually made, or how to bake a loaf of bread. To put it into perspective, my mom and I bought a tomato plant once and killed it in about a week. So, believe me when I say, I started from scratch! Why do I share this? Well, because so many of these things can seem very overwhelming, especially if you did not grow up doing them, and that can really deter people from even starting. But I promise you, it's not as intimidating as it seems. Yes, learning these skills can be hard at times, but we can do hard things! And that first time you sit down at your table to eat a truly nourishing meal made with ingredients cultivated by your own two hands, it will be one of the most rewarding feelings I think a person can experience. It connects you to your creator, to nature, and to the past in a way that can only be fully understood by experiencing it.

With that being said, hi! My name is Michelle and I am so happy you are here. Are you feeling a pull to live a more intentional life? Perhaps a life that is more connected to the Earth, more mindful of how you are nourishing your family. Although we have been sold a "hustle" lifestyle, maybe something about slowing down, getting back to your roots, and doing things the old-fashioned way is calling to your soul. That was me four short years ago. The concept of self-reliance was a term used only for people living in underground bunkers in the woods. Boy, was I wrong. In 2020, I, like many people, began to look at the way I was living and how our country operates very differently than it had before. In fall of 2019, I began showing signs of toxicity poisoning, and as I worked to heal my body, it set me on a path of learning about environmental toxins, chemicals in our products, and the harmful ingredients in our food. I realized very quickly that detoxing my body was pointless unless I started making lifestyle changes to lessen my exposure to those toxins. Now, this may seem a little off topic for a cookbook, but stay with me and I promise it will make sense. It's important to know my journey to self-reliance and the seeds of passion from which this very cookbook sprouted. One by one I began to make swaps in my skincare products, household cleaning products, cosmetics products, and most importantly, the food I bought. This journey opened my eyes to just how much our modern society is quite literally poisoning us. Fast forward to spring 2020 with the lockdowns, the empty grocery store shelves, the fear, the lack of faith in our bodies and their ability to heal, and my eyes were opened even more to how disconnected our lives are from nature and creation. Another thing that became glaringly obvious is the fact that we are not as free as we think we are and we do not have as much control as we think we do over the basic things we need to survive. I knew that God was calling me to a different way of life. I finally understood that the human body is perfectly created with incredible healing capabilities and what we need in order to nourish ourselves and ultimately thrive is already provided for us. Right here, right beneath our feet, right outside our door. If we could just silence the noise of modern society, we would stop merely living on the land and maybe, just maybe, start to *live with the land* once again, as our ancestors did.'

I know reading that may feel very heavy and will not resonate with everyone, and that's okay. I believe it's important to share my heart and be honest no matter how uncomfortable that may be. Now, don't get me wrong, I do not expect everyone reading this to quit their jobs, sell everything, move out to the woods, and start living off grid. Would that be awesome? Uh, yeah! But that's not what this book is intended to do. My intention with this book is to share, inform, inspire, and nourish. Each chapter, each lesson, each recipe is thoughtfully created to give new perspective on the way you look at food, teach you traditional cooking skills that will hopefully be passed down to the next generation, and bless you with delicious recipes that will not only nourish your family but that will allow you to make meals you are proud to put on your table each and every day. My goal is not to uproot your life or way of living, but to inspire you to root yourself in the nourishing traditions of the past that will allow your families and communities to thrive.

We may not be able to put off the future or turn back time, but we can take the wisdom of the past to make the future a better place for our children.

—xo, Michelle

Pantry

Here is what I always have on hand in my kitchen and stocked in our pantry to ensure our family is always well prepared to whip up a quick snack, dinner, or our favorite sweet treats.

Refrigerated

- Butter (salted or unsalted)
- Eggs
- Cream
- Milk
- Cream cheese
- Sour cream
- Yogurt
- Assortment of cheeses

Produce

- Bananas
- Oranges
- Strawberries
- Avocados
- Carrots
- Potatoes
- Fresh garlic
- Fresh ginger
- Onions
- Raw honey
- Fresh/dried herbs

Dry Goods

- Organic unbleached all-purpose flour
- Organic bread flour
- Organic wheat berries (for grinding own flour)
- Brown sugar (light or dark)
- Cane sugar
- Baking powder
- Baking soda
- Yeast (active dry, instant, or sourdough starter)
- Unsweetened cocoa powder
- Various chocolate chips
- Vanilla extract
- Bone broth (store-bought or homemade)
- Various nuts
- Variety of dry beans
- Rice
- Organic oats

Spices

- Sea salt
- Black pepper
- Garlic powder
- Onion powder
- Italian seasoning
- Cumin
- Paprika
- Chili powder
- Nutmeg
- Cinnamon

Cooking Oils

- Beef tallow
- Lard
- Coconut oil
- Extra virgin olive oil
- Avocado oil

Meat

- Various cuts of beef and bison
- Various cuts of chicken
- Various cuts of pork
- Wild game (from our hunts)
- Organ meat
- Breakfast sausage

Tools

Glass Measuring Cups

I use these for measuring all of my liquid ingredients as well as mixing wet ingredients such as whisking an egg or combining my BBQ sauce and ketchup mixture before pouring it on my meatloaf. I recommend Pyrex measuring cups because they are extremely durable. I have a variety of sizes ranging from 1 cup to 8 cups.

Metal Measuring Cups

A good set of measuring cups is essential, especially for baking. I prefer metal measuring cups because they are more durable, but plastic would work just fine—but always be mindful of the chemicals that can be released from plastic. A typical set ranges from ¼ cup to 1 cup.

Wooden Spoons

Call me old-fashioned, but I prefer cooking with wooden spoons over plastic or metal. For starters, they are much more durable, but you also don't have to worry about toxic chemicals such as BPA and PFAS leaching from the plastic when they get hot. As for metal utensils, these are a wonderful option, but I am not a fan of how hot they get when using, so for that reason I gravitate to wooden utensils. But keep in mind, you do need to periodically sanitize and seal the wooden utensils. You can boil them in hot water then seal them with a food safe mineral oil or beeswax.

Silicone Spatulas

Silicone spatulas are very versatile. I have a few large, medium, and small ones. I like to use these for folding in baking ingredients, making scrambled eggs, and mixing my starter feedings. They are the best for scraping the sides of the starter jar after mixing, which helps keep the jar clean.

Whisks

Whisks are pretty straightforward, but I do recommend having one of regular size and then one smaller size whisk for small volume liquid ingredients.

Metal Spatula

A metal spatula can be used for many things but I find them extremely useful for grilling, flipping pancakes, omelets, quesadillas, and transferring pizzas. They are very versatile and extremely handy in the kitchen.

Ladle

Ladles are often overlooked when it comes to kitchen utensils, but in a self-reliant kitchen a ladle is a necessity. They are used for serving soups and stews but most importantly they are used during canning. I use my ladle to transfer whatever I am canning into the jars I am using.

Tongs

If you don't already own a pair of tongs, I highly recommend getting some. I personally like to have a smaller pair of tongs for serving and cooking on the stovetop, but I also have a larger and longer pair of tongs for things like grilling or reaching down into a large pot. You don't have to have different sizes, but it can make life a little easier.

Microplane Grater

This is a tool I started using more recently. Before, I typically used a garlic press and finely chopped things like fresh ginger, but since adding this grater to my collection, my life is changed. Now it is all I use for garlic, ginger, cinnamon, Parmesan, and other things that need to be finely grated. They are incredibly easy to use, and I find myself wasting less.

Box Grater

This is another self-explanatory tool and almost every kitchen already has one, but none-theless, I wanted to include it. This grater is a must for me because I am not a fan of store-bought shredded cheeses, mostly because they are usually filled with preservatives and anti-caking ingredients that I like to keep out of my menu. So I typically freshly grate all of my cheeses, especially when I've made homemade cheese from scratch. It is also great for grating veggies.

Rolling Pin

When it comes to a rolling pin, some will say use a marble, others will say use wood. Here is what I have to say on the topic: I personally use a wood roller, not because I think it's better, but just because it's what I have. So, feel free to use whatever type of rolling pin you are comfortable with. I will say a marble rolling pin is easier to keep clean because it is such a smooth surface, but use what works for you, your kitchen, and your budget. But for a self-reliant kitchen, just make sure you have one as you will be using it a lot!

Vegetable Peeler

Once again, I feel like this is very self-explanatory and most kitchens already have one of some sort.

Stainless Steel Masher

This is most commonly known as a potato masher. Growing up, I used a hand-held mixer to make mashed potatoes, but when my husband and I started dating, he only had a "potato masher," so that's what I started using. Nine years later I am still using that same potato masher. There is something so soothing about mashing your potatoes by hand, and it gives them the most amazing texture and consistency.

Chef's Knife

In a self-reliant kitchen you will be doing a lot of chopping, so having a great quality chef's knife will be incredibly helpful. There is nothing worse than chopping vegetables with a poor quality knife. There are a lot of styles, so choose what you like best. I personally source from craftsmen who make knives by hand. They do tend to be more expensive, but the quality and durability is unmatched and supporting local businesses is a huge priority for me, but do not feel like you need to spend a fortune on a knife set. Find one that works within your budget that you like using.

Paring Knife

A paring knife is a small knife with a curved blade that fits snugly in your hand. I use my paring knife daily for things like cutting fruit, trimming vegetables, small amounts of peeling, and slicing butter or cheeses.

Bread Knife

A good bread knife is extremely useful in a self-reliant kitchen. There are tons of styles of bread knives out there, but my personal favorite is the Bow Bread Knife. I don't know if they work better or if I just think they look cool, but either way, I just recommend a bread knife of some sort. It will be your best friend while you are baking your heart out!

Pastry Cutter

This U-shaped tool with a handle and thin metal slats is used to cut cold, solid fat such as butter or shortening into flour for things such as pastries, biscuits, etc.

Mixing Bowls

You can never have too many mixing bowls. Well, maybe you can—I probably have too many. However, I have a mixture of sizes and types. My mixing bowls range from small, like the size of a cereal bowl, to very large. It's important to have a variety of sizes for the variety of needs that you will have. I also have metal, ceramic, and glass mixing bowls. In my opinion, one material isn't better than the other, I just like variety. Just keep in mind what you are using them for and if they are microwave safe.

Mason Jars

I can't emphasize this one enough! I use mason jars for so many different things—canning, food storage, sourdough starter, cups, storing used eggshells, meal prep containers, and so much more. I like to have a variety of sizes from small to extremely large. Ball is definitely my preferred brand, but there are a lot of great ones. A good money-saving tip is to check out your local thrift store—they usually have them for very cheap. Just be sure to wash them well before use. If you're planning on canning, just inspect them for any cracks or chips, and I always use new lids.

Pie Pan/Plate

Pie plates are a must in my kitchen. I use them for pies, obviously, but they also make great dredging dishes when you're preparing fried food and need to coat something with eggs, flour, or breading. There are many options for disposable pie plate options, but from a sustainability and self-reliance standpoint, I like to have reusable dishes such as glass, metal, or ceramic.

Cast Iron Pan

If someone asked me what my go-to cooking pan would be, I would say cast iron. I use my cast iron skillet every single day. I do everything from scrambled eggs and fried chicken to baking

and heating up tortillas. They can even go right on an open fire. You can't get more homestead than that! Cast irons are very easy to clean. You can use a metal abrasive scrubber, but often, depending on what I cooked, I'll just use a traditional sponge or brush. After cleaning, it's very important to place back on heat to dry completely and then rub it down with cooking oil to prevent rusting. I recommend having a few different sizes and depths for versatility.

Tall Stock Pot

This is another item I would say every kitchen needs. In terms of self-reliance, a tall stock pot allows you to do many things in the kitchen that you would otherwise outsource. I make large batches of soups, stews, and chilies in mine and then freeze, dehydrate, or can leftovers. I also make all of my homemade bone broths in them, as well as different types of homeopathic remedies that call for boiling herbs and such (I have a separate stock pot for this). And finally, you use them to water bath can.

Canners

There are three main types of canners: pressure canners, steam canners, and water bath canners. A pressure canner is used for canning low acid vegetables and meat. Don't confuse a pressure canner with a pressure cooker like the Instant Pot. Water bath and steam canners are just two different caning methods for similar types of foods, fruits, high acidic vegetables like tomatoes, pickled products, and jams/jellies. A water bath and steam canner can be interchangeable for the most part. However, if a recipe calls for a processing/canning time of longer than 45 minutes, steam canning is not recommended due to the possibility of it boiling dry.

Dutch Oven

Dutch ovens are one of my favorite cooking dishes. Like my cast iron pan, I use this for so many different things, but the most important one to note is, I bake my sourdough loaves in my Dutch oven. If you do not already have a Dutch oven, I strongly encourage you to get one. You will use it more than you think.

Deep Casserole Dish

Being from Michigan, I have to include a casserole dish. Man, we love our casseroles in the Midwest. Either glass or ceramic is fine. Casserole dishes are so versatile, and I especially love them for making dishes for potlucks or parties; they typically come with a lid, so they transport easily and double as a serving dish as well.

Loaf Pan

Being self-reliant in the kitchen means making your own bread, so owning a good quality loaf pan is essential. My favorite brand is USA PAN. They're great quality and hold up wonderfully. When you bake as much as I do, you need something durable.

Muffin & Cake Pans

I put these together because I think they go hand in hand. When I set out to live a more self-reliant lifestyle, I ditched store-bought baked goods, especially muffins and cakes. I recommend having a few different sizes for each.

Baking Sheet

Baking sheets don't really need an explanation, but it's safe to say I use a baking sheet almost every day. Mine are very old and not fancy in any way, but they do the job. Nowadays they come in a variety of materials and styles. Choose what you like and what works for you.

Wire Cooling Rack

Until a few years ago, I had never owned a cooling rack. Let me tell you, they're a game changer. Not only do I use it as a cooling rack for baked sweets, but I also use it when I'm baking or air frying meats or vegetables. I place my wire rack on a baking sheet and place whatever I am cooking—potatoes, chicken tenders, veggies, etc.—on the wire rack. Placing them on the rack instead of just the sheet pan allows the air to circulate, allowing them to cook more evenly, creating a crispier finish.

Fine Mesh Strainer

This may be a less common item, but I think it is a very useful tool. Some of the things I use my mesh strainer for are draining fat from ground meat, sifting flour, and straining fruit preserves.

Flour Sifter

Many baking recipes call for sifted flour, and although there are ways to sift flour without a true sifter, these sure make life a lot easier. Most flour sifters are pretty inexpensive and can be found at grocery or home goods stores. You can even find some at thrift stores if you keep an eye out.

Food Processor

Food processors will vary in size from small to very large. I personally have a medium-size one that meets the needs of our family. A food processor is an incredibly versatile tool. In ours I typically make hummus, pesto, grind nuts, and make batches of salsa.

Electric Stand Mixer

A good and sturdy stand mixer is very useful for someone who loves to bake as much as I do. In addition to baking, I also use my stand mixer for making fresh homemade butter, whipped cream, and even pasta (using the pasta attachments). It also comes in handy if you make a lot of bread or you're short on time, since a stand mixer can reduce your kneading time drastically by using the dough hook on a low speed. The stand mixer I currently have is a KitchenAid and I opt for the stainless-steel attachments.

Handheld Mixer

My stand mixer is great for larger jobs, but if I need to mix up a small batch of something quickly, I will use my hand mixer.

Cutting Boards

I prefer wood cutting boards over plastic ones. In my experience, wood cutting boards hold up better, especially if you are taking care of them and periodically conditioning them. I generally avoid plastic cutting boards because I don't find them as durable and also because of the potential chemical release from them. Plus, I just prefer to use natural materials. Once again, I try to find local craftsmen that make them by hand so I can support their businesses. However, whether you are using wood or plastic cutting boards, I recommend cutting boards that have a groove around the edge to help catch liquids from spilling onto the counter.

Parchment Paper

Parchment paper is a must for me when it comes to baking. I line my baking sheets with it when I'm baking cookies. I make my own muffin liners with it, and I use it when I'm making sourdough bread. I place my unbaked, scored loaf of sourdough on a large piece of parchment paper and place that in my Dutch oven. When it comes to choosing parchment paper, I personally opt for an unbleached option.

Ingredient Sourcing

How we source our food is just as important as the ingredients in our food. As you dive into this book, you will realize I will always advocate for "as local as possible," and the most local place you can source your food from is right in your own backyard. That is why I strongly encourage starting a garden, whether that is a couple pots on your windowsill with a few herbs or a full blown garden or greenhouse. Whatever is feasible for you, go for it! Similarly, one of the best ways to start having your own food source is to get some backyard chickens (laying hens) to have fresh eggs every day. Thankfully, chickens do not require a ton of space like many other animals, and they are relatively low maintenance. As long as they have a clean coop, some space to range freely, and fresh water and food, they are good to go. A garden and chickens are my go-to recommendations for beginners wanting to be a little more self-reliant with their food sourcing. Now, what about all the other stuff? Because let's face it, most of us don't just eat vegetables and eggs. What is the best practice for shopping for all of the other food we eat? Source local as much as you can. Keep reading for more specific tips.

How do I find local produce if I don't have a garden?

Sourcing local produce is a little bit easier than sourcing local meat, in my opinion. Search for organic farms and local co-ops in your area that you can buy directly from. Many of them do memberships where you pay a set fee and every week or every other week you pick up a box of freshly harvested produce. This method of produce sourcing is typically much cheaper than buying from chain grocery stores and is a great way to eat seasonally. I always encourage sourcing organic when possible, especially when purchasing high pesticide foods like strawberries, apples, potatoes, tomatoes, and many others. You can look up "the dirty dozen" to learn which fruits and vegetables have the highest amounts of pesticide residue. Farmers' markets are another great way to shop locally for your produce.

How do I source local meat?

A great place to start is your local butcher shop. However, not every butcher shop will only have local meat, so don't be afraid to ask and shop around until you find the quality of meat you are happy with. You can also visit farmers' markets. After that, I would suggest simply typing into your web browser, "locally raised meat (*insert state or city*)." You may be surprised at how many resources pop up. As the saying goes, "you are what your food eats," so always look into how the animals are raised and what they are fed. If you are lucky to find a local direct-to-consumer farm, feel free to ask if you can stop by the farm to see for yourself how the animals are raised. This is also a great way to build a deeper connection with your food and learn more about the farm-to-table process, which is especially great if you have kiddos. If you have the budget and freezer space, I recommend purchasing larger portions of meat like a full cow, ½ cow, or ¼ cow. This also applies to most other animals. Although the price tag may seem big, you actually get the most bang for your buck and then you are set for the rest of the year or longer, which makes my little self-reliant heart sing.

What is regenerative agriculture and why is it important?

Regenerative agriculture is farming and ranching practices that focus on the health of the ecological system as a whole. Modern industrial farming practices have placed focus on creating the highest yield crop at the expense of the soil health. Regenerative agriculture aims to restore the health and vitality of our soil, increase biodiversity, reduce waste, and create more sustainable farming practices that are more aligned with the biocompatibility of the land. The reason this is so important is because much of our soil is depleted of minerals and nutrients, leaving what we consume void of those nutrients and creating deficiencies within the human body, which can lead to a plethora of health issues. Regenerative practices work towards restoring the soil health of our land, which will have a ripple effect to our overall health and the health of our ecosystem.

Eggs: cage-free vs. free-range vs. pasture-raised

At grocery stores you'll often see many different classifications of eggs. What do these labels actually mean? "Cage-free" and "free-range" have to do with how the hens are raised. In industrial farming, many hens are packed into small cages with little to no room for movement and no access to outside. "Cage-free" means the chicken can move more freely but may still not have access to outdoor areas. "Free-range" is classified as having some outdoor time, but there is no standard in place that specifies how much outside time is needed to be classified as free-range. Pasture-raised, my preference for store-bought eggs, is the highest quality level when it comes to animal welfare. Pasture-raised hens typically have more indoor space per hen and continuous access to covered or uncovered outdoor vegetation to roam and forage. If you don't have the ability to raise your own chickens, farmers' markets are a great way to buy local eggs.

CHAPTER 1

Sourdough and Yeast Breads

Sourdough Starter

One of the biggest staples of a self-reliant kitchen is a sourdough starter. All you need is flour and water and you will always be able to have fresh bread on hand. A sourdough starter can be temperamental, but with practice and a little patience I have no doubt you will be able to have a thriving starter for years to come.

Day 1: Add 1 tablespoon unbleached all-purpose flour or whole wheat flour with 1 tablespoon lukewarm filtered water in a clean jar and mix thoroughly. Cover and let sit in a warm spot for 24 hours.

Day 2: Add to same jar 1 tablespoon flour with 1 tablespoon lukewarm filtered water and mix thoroughly. Cover and let sit in a warm spot for 24 hours.

Day 3: Remove 1 tablespoon of starter and add to a clean jar. Add in 1 tablespoon flour and 1 tablespoon lukewarm filtered water and mix thoroughly. Cover and let sit 24 hours.

Day 4: Remove 1 tablespoon of starter and add to a clean jar. Add in 2 tablespoons flour and 2 tablespoons lukewarm filtered water and mix thoroughly. Cover and let sit 24 hours.

Day 5: At this point, you should start to see some bubbles forming and it should be rising a little bit. Remove 1 tablespoon of starter and add to a clean jar. Add in ¼ cup flour and ¼ cup lukewarm filtered water and mix thoroughly. Cover and let sit 24 hours. (If your starter is on the runny side, use a tiny bit less water than flour to achieve a consistency a little thicker than pancake batter).

Day 6: Remove 1 tablespoon of starter and add to a clean jar. Add in ¼ cup flour and ¼ cup lukewarm filtered water and mix thoroughly. Cover and let sit 24 hours. (At this point, starter should have lots of tiny bubbles and rise a decent bit between each feeding, though it won't quite be doubling in size).

Day 7–10: Repeat steps for Day 6.

Day 11: At this point, your starter should double in size after 12 hours and you are ready to bake.

(Continued on next page)

NOTES

*Keep in mind that starters like warmer temperatures, ideally around 76°F/24°C. If you have a cooler house, try to find a spot tucked away that is warmer. For me, that is on top of my fridge pushed against the back (heat from the fridge radiates upward). You can also try inside the oven with just the light on.

*If you are using whole wheat flour, those starters typically become much more active a lot more quickly than when using all-purpose flour, so your timeline may speed up.

*When feeding my starter, I like to keep it a little on the thicker side. I find that I get better activity from the starter than when it is runnier. To achieve this, I add my water a little bit at a time and mix in between until I reach my desired consistency.

*You know your starter is ready to start baking with when it doubles or more in size after 12 hours. You'll want to feed your starter about 12 hours before the time you want to start baking (I typically feed my starter before I go to bed so it is ready in the morning).

*Even if you don't plan on baking with it, I recommend feeding it once a day while it is still a new starter.

*Keep a starter discard jar to make yummy discard recipes with.

Beginner Sourdough Loaf

Yield: *1 Loaf*

Beginning your sourdough journey can seem a little daunting and that is why I created this easy-to-follow beginner sourdough recipe. This simple recipe will make one delicious sourdough loaf. If you have a larger family or want to make more than one loaf, you can easily double this recipe.

Note: *Feed your starter about 12 hours before you plan to begin baking with it.*

Ingredients

125 grams (1 cup) active starter

367 grams (1½ cups) filtered water

500 grams (4 cups) unbleached all-purpose flour

12 grams (2 teaspoons) salt

Instructions

1. Combine active starter, water, and flour together in a large bowl. Mix with a spoon until fully incorporated and a shaggy dough forms. Cover with a towel or plate and let rest for 30 minutes.
2. In a small bowl, combine salt with 1 teaspoon of water. Mix well and pour over dough.
3. Gently work salt into dough by pressing down with fingertips. Then perform a set of stretch and folds (see note on page 7 and check out my sourdough tutorial videos on my Instagram: @itsmichellerae_). Cover and let rest for 30 minutes.
4. After 30 minutes, perform another set of stretch and folds. Cover and let rest. Repeat this process every 30 minutes three more times.
5. Cover bowl and set aside for 12 hours to allow a bulk ferment.
6. After 12 hours, remove dough from bowl and place onto a clean, lightly floured surface and begin to laminate the dough (stretch out flat). Once stretched out, fold the sides over the middle. Then, starting at one end, roll the dough into a ball. Then begin gently working the dough by sliding the dough forward and back to create tension.
7. Place dough into a well-floured sourdough proofing basket. If you don't have a proofing basket, you could use a three- or four-quart mixing bowl, lined with a cheese cloth and well floured. (Place dough upside down so the smooth top is facing down in the basket).

(Continued on page 7)

8. Cover and place in fridge for at least 2 hours (I like to cover with a disposable shower cap, but you can use a plastic grocery bag, too).
9. After 2 hours, preheat oven to 450°F. Place Dutch oven in oven while preheating to get hot.
10. Once preheated, place loaf on parchment paper and score the loaf by making a slit across the top. Carefully remove hot Dutch oven and place scored loaf in the Dutch oven. Cover with lid and bake for 25 minutes.
11. After 25 minutes, remove the lid and continue baking for 15 minutes.
12. Carefully remove from oven, take out loaf, and set aside to completely cool before slicing.
13. Store in a bread bag, bread box, or cover well with a towel and leave out on counter to enjoy. Once sliced, loaf will last about 5 days.

NOTES

Stretch and fold: To perform a stretch and fold, grab the edge of one side of the dough, gently pull and stretch it upward and fold it over onto itself. Repeat this process on each side of the dough for a total of four times.

Storage: If you want to make multiple sourdough loaves and store them for the future, you can slice your loaf and place those slices in a freezer bag and freeze for later.

Sourdough English Muffins

Yield: *18–20 muffins*

There is nothing I love more than an English muffin with my breakfast. I start the process about 24 hours before I plan to cook them. Example timeline: 8 a.m. I feed my starter; 8 p.m. I make the dough and let rise overnight; 8 a.m. next day I portion the dough and cook them.

Ingredients

TO MAKE THE STARTER

40 grams (about 2 tablespoons) sourdough starter

120 grams (1 cup) unbleached all-purpose flour

85 grams (⅓ cup) water

TO MAKE THE DOUGH

200 grams (1 cup) active sourdough starter

720 grams (6 cups) unbleached all-purpose flour

2 cups milk

2 tablespoons honey

2 teaspoons salt

Cornmeal for sprinkling

Instructions

1. About 12 hours before you plan to make the dough, feed your starter.
2. Transfer starter, flour, and water into a clean jar. Mix thoroughly, cover loosely, and put in a warm place for 12 hours.
3. Once your starter has doubled in size (about 12 hours later), place the active starter, flour, milk, honey, and salt in the bowl of an electric stand mixer.
4. Roughly mix ingredients by hand, then attach dough hook and mix on speed 2 for about 5 minutes or until dough is soft and elastic. Should no longer stick to edges of bowl.
5. Once mixed, transfer to a clean bowl, cover with plastic wrap (I use a shower cap), and leave on counter to rise for 12 hours (I let rise overnight).
6. Turn out the dough onto a floured surface. Sprinkle flour over top and gently roll out to 1-inch thickness with rolling pin. (If you don't have a rolling pin, press out with fingertips.)
7. Then use a biscuit cutter (I like to use a 3-inch cutter, but any round cutter will work—even a coffee mug). Place rounds onto a piece of parchment paper, either on a baking sheet or the countertop, and sprinkle with cornmeal. Cover with a tea towel and let rise for about 1 hour.
8. Preheat skillet on low heat. Place muffins in skillet about 2 inches apart. Cover and cook for 5 minutes on first side. Turn muffins over and cook another 5 minutes. (Internal temperature should read 200°F)
9. Once finished, place on a cooling rack to cool and repeat process with remaining muffins.

Sourdough Cinnamon Raisin Bread

Yield: *1 Loaf*

There is nothing more delicious than a fresh slice of cinnamon raisin bread smothered in warm, melty butter. I'm drooling just thinking about it. This bread will definitely be a crowd-pleaser, especially if you have kiddos. For this recipe you will need a 9 × 5-inch loaf pan.

Ingredients

280 grams (2 cups) bread flour

180 grams (1½ cups) unbleached all-purpose flour

250 grams (1 cup) sourdough starter

1 cup whole milk

2 tablespoons honey

2 tablespoons maple syrup

3 tablespoons sugar

3 tablespoons cinnamon, divided

1 cup raisins

1 tablespoon butter

1 teaspoon sea salt

Instructions

DAY 1:

1. Morning: feed your starter. I typically feed my starter about 12 hours before I want to use it in a recipe.
2. Evening: In a stand mixer fitted with dough hook, add both flours, active starter, milk, honey, maple syrup, sugar, and 1 tablespoon cinnamon in bowl and mix on low-medium speed until its smooth and elastic. *If you don't have a stand mixer, add to a bowl and knead by hand.*
3. Cover the dough and let rise overnight.

DAY 2:

1. In the morning, put raisins in a bowl, cover with warm water for 10–15 minutes, then strain off the water.
2. Butter your 9 × 5-inch loaf pan and set aside.
3. Lightly flour your work surface and turn dough out onto it. Gently shape the dough into a rectangle. Lightly dust your rolling pin and top of dough with flour and roll out until about ½-inch thick.
4. Evenly spread remaining 2 tablespoons cinnamon and raisins over dough to completely cover it.
5. Starting at the top of the dough, gently roll the dough into a tight log, then fold the ends towards the middle and give it a gentle roll to help seal the loaf.
6. Place loaf into pan, cover, and let rise until double in size. Depending on temperature of room, mine typically takes 2–4 hours.
7. Bake loaf at 400°F for 30 minutes or until internal temperature is 195°F.
8. Remove bread from pan and let cool completely on cooling rack.
9. Once cooled, slice and enjoy!

Sourdough Sandwich Loaf

Yield: *1 loaf*

Once you start making your own sandwich bread, you won't want to go back to store-bought again. Every Sunday or every other Sunday, I do a bread restock for my family. I make this recipe, my sourdough loaf, and a batch of English muffins for the upcoming week. In addition to having delicious and healthy bread, who doesn't love a kitchen filled with the aroma of fresh baked bread?

Note: *This is the same recipe I use for my hamburger buns and dinner rolls.*

Ingredients

500 grams (4 cups) unbleached all-purpose flour

4 tablespoons unsalted butter, softened at room temperature

1 tablespoon sugar

1 teaspoon sea salt

50 grams (¼ cup) active, bubbly sourdough starter

270 grams (1 cup) water, lukewarm

Instructions

NIGHT BEFORE:

1. In a bowl, mix together flour, butter, sugar, and salt until the mixture becomes crumbly. I like to do this step by hand, but you could use a stand mixer with a paddle attachment.
2. Add in active starter and lukewarm water. Mix by hand until fully mixed. Dough should be sticky at this stage. Cover with plastic wrap (I like to use a disposable shower cap) and let rest for 30 minutes.
3. Once rested, transfer dough to the bowl of a stand mixer fitted with a dough hook. Knead dough on low-medium speed (#2 or #3) for about 8 minutes. At this point, the dough should be soft and elastic. If dough is sticky, add in a little flour and continue kneading.
4. Cover and let rest overnight, about 12 hours.

NEXT MORNING:

1. Butter loaf pan and set aside.
2. Turn dough out onto a lightly floured work surface and gently flatten into a rectangle, working out any air bubbles.
3. Shape and roll dough into a log shape, starting with the sides, then folding over the ends. Then gently cup and pull the dough towards you to create a tight loaf (same motion as when making a traditional sourdough loaf).
4. Place dough seam-side down in loaf pan, cover, and let rest about 2 hours. Dough should rise above sides of pan.
5. Bake at 375°F for 50 minutes. Allow to cool in pan for about 10–15 minutes, then transfer to cooling rack.

Sourdough Bagels

Yield: *8 servings*

Bagels are such an easy and delicious breakfast addition, and homemade sourdough bagels knock anything you could buy from the store out of the water. I have included everything bagel seasoning as my bagel topping, but you can top your bagel with whatever style/flavor you like.

Ingredients

DOUGH

155 grams (¾ cup) active sourdough starter

250 grams (1 cup + 1 tablespoon) warm filtered water

2 tablespoons granulated sugar or honey, divided

1½ teaspoons fine sea salt

500 grams (4 cups + 2 tablespoons) bread flour

Everything bagel seasoning, optional

1 tablespoon sugar for water boil

Instructions

To have fresh bagels in the morning, follow this timeline:

1. Around 8 a.m. on the day before, feed your starter, enough to create at least 1 cup of starter. (See page 3 for instructions on how to feed your starter.)
2. At 8 p.m., when your starter is active and bubbly, make your bagel dough. In the mixing bowl of your stand mixer or just a medium-large mixing bowl, combine starter, water, 1 tablespoon sugar or honey, and salt.
3. Add in bread flour. Then, using your hands, bring the ingredients together until a shaggy dough forms.
4. If using a stand mixer, use the dough hook and work the dough on low speed for 6–8 minutes until the dough pulls away from the sides and becomes soft and supple. If using hands, knead dough for about 10–12 minutes.
5. Cover bowl and let sit at room temperature for 8–12 hours (overnight).
6. In the morning, line a baking sheet with parchment paper.
7. Turn dough out onto clean work surface (if dough is sticky, I like to wet my fingertips a little). Cut into 8 equal pieces. Start with one piece of dough and poke a hole in the middle. Then, using your fingers, work the dough into a bagel shape. Place down on the parchment paper and repeat with remaining bagels. Cover with a towel and let rise another 30 minutes, until they puff up, almost doubling in size (if your kitchen is colder, this may take up to 1 hour).
8. Preheat oven to 425°F. Fill up a pot with water, add 1 tablespoon sugar, and bring to a boil.
9. Place each bagel in the boiling water for 2 minutes on each side. (I like to use a mesh strainer to place and remove them from the water.) *Only boil 3–4 at a time to avoid over-crowding the pot.*
10. Once done boiling, place back on parchment paper and top as desired. I like to dip some in everything bagel seasoning and leave some plain.
11. After you top them and place back on the baking sheet with parchment paper, bake for 20–25 minutes or until golden brown.
12. Store in a sealed container or a bread bag if you have one.

Sourdough Buns

Yield: *10–12 Buns*

These soft, fluffy hamburger buns are the perfect addition to your summer BBQs. If you want to take your hamburger bun game to the next level, toast them on the grill before serving. This is the same recipe I use for my sandwich bread with the addition of the egg wash mixture.

Ingredients

500 grams (4 cups) unbleached all-purpose flour

4 tablespoons unsalted butter, softened at room temperature

1 tablespoon sugar

1 teaspoon sea salt

50 grams (¼ cup) active, bubbly sourdough starter

270 grams (1 cup) water, lukewarm

1 egg

1 tablespoon water

Instructions

NIGHT BEFORE:

1. In a bowl, mix together flour, butter, sugar, and salt until the mixture becomes crumbly. I like to do this step by hand, but you could use a stand mixer with a paddle attachment.
2. Add in active starter and lukewarm water. Mix thoroughly by hand. Dough should be sticky at this stage. Cover with plastic wrap (I like to use a disposable shower cap) and let rest for 30 minutes.
3. Once rested, transfer dough to bowl of a stand mixer fitted with a dough hook. Knead dough on low-medium speed (#2 or #3) for about 8 minutes. At this point, the dough should be soft and elastic. If dough is sticky, add in a little flour and continue kneading.
4. Cover and let rest overnight, about 12 hours.

NEXT DAY:

1. Place dough onto a lightly floured surface and gently press out into a rectangle.
2. Cut the dough into 8 even sections. Once cut, take each section and form dough into a ball. Take the outer edges of the dough and softly pull them into the middles to form the ball. Then gently work the dough as needed until a tight ball is formed. You want a little tension in the dough.
3. Once all of the dough balls are formed, place them on a large lightly-floured sheet pan and cover and let rise until double in size.
4. Preheat oven to 350°F.
5. Beat the egg and water together, then brush the tops of the buns. (If desired, sprinkle with sesame seeds or a little everything bagel seasoning.)
6. Bake the buns for 30 minutes or until golden on top.

Sourdough Pizza Dough

Yield: *4 crusts*

This recipe has quickly become a favorite in our household. The flavor and texture of the crust once it's baked is incredible—the perfect amount of chew and crunch. This is a recipe I like to double or even triple to freeze. If you want to try this, wrap the portion of dough in plastic wrap, then place in a freezer bag and store in freezer for up to a few months.

Ingredients

125 grams (1 cup) active sourdough starter

367 grams (1½ cups) filtered water

500 grams (4 cups) unbleached all-purpose flour

2 teaspoons salt

2 teaspoons olive oil

Instructions

1. The morning of pizza night, add all ingredients into the bowl of your stand mixer fitted with the dough hook attachment. Mix all ingredients on low-medium speed for about 10 minutes. (The dough should be soft and elastic.)
2. Transfer to an oiled bowl, cover with plastic wrap or lid, and let rest for about 8 hours.
3. Preheat oven to 475°F. (Pro tip: I like to cook my pizza on a heated pizza stone or cast iron skillet. It really helps create the crispy crust texture.)
4. Turn dough out onto lightly floured surface and divide into 4 equal parts. Gently roll and stretch out the dough into a pizza shape. I like to create a slight ridge around the edge for the traditional pizza crust.
5. Spread sauce onto pizza. (Check out my marinara recipe on page 85; it is the perfect pizza sauce recipe.)
6. Add your favorite toppings.
7. Bake for about 15 minutes and finish off with a broil on low for a couple minutes. This extra step gives you the perfect crisp on the edge of the crust. (If you are finding your dough is a little undercooked in the center, you can do a pre-bake before putting your toppings on. Bake the dough for 8 minutes, remove from oven, add your favorite toppings, return to oven for another 5–8 minutes, then switch to broiler for a few minutes.)

Sweet Dinner Rolls

Yield: *12 Rolls*

These sweet dinner rolls are my go-to for every holiday dinner. They are like little pillowy balls of buttery goodness, so soft and fluffy. Man, my mouth is watering just thinking about them! I promise they will be the biggest hit at your next Thanksgiving dinner.

Note: *If you do not have a stand mixer, the dough can be mixed and kneaded by hand.*

Ingredients

½ cup milk

¼ cup butter

½ cup sugar

1 teaspoon salt

½ cup warm water

2 packages active dry yeast

2 eggs, beaten

4½ cups all-purpose flour

Instructions

1. First bring milk to a boil, then immediately remove from heat and stir in butter, sugar, and salt. Set aside and cool to room temperature.
2. In a stand mixer, add warm water and yeast. Let sit for a few minutes, then add in milk mixture and mix thoroughly until all yeast is dissolved.
3. Add in beaten eggs and mix thoroughly.
4. Attach dough hook to stand mixer. Add in flour and mix on low-medium speed for about 5–8 minutes.
5. Transfer to a buttered bowl, cover bowl, and let rise until doubled in size. Should take about an hour, depending on temperature of room.
6. Once doubled in size, punch down and turn out onto a lighly-floured surface.
7. Separate into 12 equal pieces of dough and form dough into balls.
8. Place into a buttered baking dish about 1–2 inches apart. Cover and let rise for about 1 hour. You will want the balls of dough to double in size again.
9. Bake at 350°F for 20–25 minutes.
10. Remove from oven and immediately brush with melted butter.
11. Allow rolls to cool about 8–10 minutes and enjoy!

Crescent Rolls

Yield: *24 servings*

Warm, soft, flakey crescent rolls are a great accompaniment for many dishes and occasions. You can also add cocktail wieners to each dough triangle before rolling them up to make pigs in a blanket.

Ingredients

1 cup warm milk

½ cup (1 stick) melted butter

1 tablespoon sugar

1 tablespoon instant yeast

2 cups all-purpose flour

1 tablespoon butter for brushing tops

Instructions

1. Start by making the dough. In small saucepan, warm milk, butter, and sugar until melted. Pour into the mixing bowl of your stand mixer fitted with dough hook. (Mixture should be warm or lukewarm.) If mixing by hand, pour into large mixing bowl. Stir in yeast and wait 1–2 minutes.

2. Slowly add in flour, mixing on low speed until dough forms a soft ball that pulls away from the sides of the bowl. If mixing by hand, place dough on lightly floured surface and knead for 6–8 minutes. Place dough in greased bowl, cover, and let rise 1–2 hours until doubled in size.

3. Preheat oven to 350°F.

4. Once dough is doubled in size, punch down and turn out onto lightly floured surface. Divided into 2 halves and roll out into roughly 9 × 13-inch rectangles. Cut each sheet of dough into 12 equal-sized triangles.

5. Starting at the wide end of each, roll dough to create a crescent roll shape. Place on sheet pan lined with parchment paper and bake 15–20 minutes or until golden brown on top.

CHAPTER 2

Dairy

Home-Churned Butter

Yield: *1 pint of cream will make 1 cup of butter*

Homemade butter is one of the simplest staples of a self-reliant kitchen. It only has one ingredient and you literally cannot mess it up. Most store-bought butters are filled with vegetable oils and other unhealthy ingredients, so I highly recommend making a swap for homemade butter.

Ingredients

Raw cream (see notes)

Salt (optional)

Instructions

1. In a stand mixer fitted with the whisk attachment, pour cream into mixing bowl.
2. Set to high speed and mix until butter forms (12–15 minutes). As you're mixing, you will see the cream pass though the "whipped cream" phase, then begin to separate, then the butter fat solids will fully separate, leaving behind a liquid (buttermilk).
3. Place butter into a bowl with ice water. Rinse under cold water while squeezing with your hand to remove all milky liquid. When it gets too soft, place back into ice water until it firms up. Then rinse and squeeze again.
4. Once liquid running out of butter is clear, shape as you'd like and place in sealed container (I like using glass containers). If you want salted butter, sprinkle in a little salt during the shaping process.

NOTES

I prefer raw cream because it is a great source of essential vitamins and minerals, helps strengthen your immune system, and contains beneficial bacterial which is helpful with digestion. And the fact that it's cream in its purest form. But you can use pasteurized cream if you prefer (I still recommend sourcing an organic, grass-fed cream if possible). Raw dairy products may contain dangerous bacteria, so do what you feel is best for you and your family.

If you do not own a stand mixer, you can just place the cream in a mason jar, seal tightly, and shake or place in a blender and blend on medium-high speed until the butter fat separates from the buttermilk.

Chocolate Milk

Yield: *1 serving*

Once you try this recipe you will never buy chocolate milk at the store again! I prefer to use raw milk due to its added nutrients, but pasteurized milk will also work fine. Raw dairy products may contain dangerous bacteria, so do what you feel is best for you and your family.

Ingredients

1 cup milk (I prefer raw milk)

1–2 tablespoons unsweetened cocoa powder

1 tablespoon pure maple syrup

½ teaspoon vanilla

Instructions

1. Pour milk, cocoa powder, maple syrup, and vanilla into blender.
2. Place lid on top and blend until fully mixed (about 10–15 seconds).
3. Drink and enjoy. That's literally it!

Homemade Mozzarella

Yield: *8 ounces*

After making homemade mozzarella, I promise you will not want to go back to store-bought. When I first started making mozzarella from scratch, I was pleasantly surprised at how easy it actually was. Keep in mind you will need a good kitchen/ food/candy thermometer.

Ingredients

1 gallon milk (I like to use raw*)

1½ teaspoons citric acid or lemon juice

¼ teaspoon animal or vegetable rennet
(I used animal rennet)

1 teaspoon salt

Instructions

1. Add milk and citric acid or lemon juice to a large pot and heat on medium. Bring to 88°F.
2. While milk is being brought to temperature, mix animal rennet with a little water to dissolve in a small dish. Once milk reaches 88°F, pour in rennet mixture and gently stir.
3. Bring to 105°F, then remove from heat and let sit for about 10 minutes (you will see the cheese curd form in the pot). While you are waiting, prepare a bowl lined with cheesecloth.
4. After 10 minutes, using a knife, cut the curd in a grid pattern and scoop into the cheesecloth. Once all the curd is transferred, gather the end of the cheesecloth to form a bag-like structure, then gently squeeze out some of the liquid.
5. Now hang the cheesecloth bag for 25–40 minutes until no more liquid is dripping. (I tie my cheesecloth to my cabinet with a bowl underneath.)
6. Once fully drained, heat the remaining liquid (whey) to 150°–200°F. Remove cheese from the cloth and add in salt. Gently work the salt into cheese.
7. Once liquid is brought to temperature, put on some type of heat-resistant gloves and gather the cheese into a ball. Begin dunking the cheese into the hot liquid while gently performing stretch and folds of the cheese until it is soft, silky, and elastic like mozzarella from the store. Form into a ball and place in a sealable glass container with a little bit of the liquid whey. Store in fridge.

---

* Raw dairy products may contain dangerous bacteria.

Yogurt

Yield: *about 10 cups*

Homemade yogurt is so delicious and so stinking easy to make. If you have an Instant Pot, all you do is add the ingredients together and press the yogurt button. Seriously, that's it! I love a loaded yogurt bowl for breakfast. Add some granola, bee pollen, fruit, and honey and you have a breakfast jam-packed with nutrients. It's also a great nighttime snack if you're craving something sweet but do not want to indulge in the usual cookie or ice cream-type dessert.

Ingredients

1 gallon whole milk (I prefer to use raw*)

1 cup yogurt starter (see notes)

Instructions

1. First, thoroughly clean the stainless-steel insert for your Instant Pot.
2. Add raw milk (or milk of choice) and yogurt starter into Instant Pot insert. Whisk together, place the lid on, and hit yogurt button twice.
3. Set timer for 24 hours.
4. Once time is up, remove the lid and stir yogurt.
5. Make sure to remove 1 cup of the yogurt and place in a tightly sealed jar to inoculate for your next batch of yogurt (this is your yogurt starter).
6. Place remaining yogurt into glass container and place in fridge for 24 hours to set. Then enjoy with your favorite toppings!

NOTES

You can use 1 cup of store-bought full-fat plain yogurt for your starter, 1 cup of previously made homemade yogurt, or purchase yogurt starter cultures (Cultures for Health is one of my favorite brands).

Homemade yogurt will tend to have a runnier consistency than what you are used to from a store-bought yogurt. If you prefer a thicker, creamier consistency, you can strain the yogurt through multiple layers of cheesecloth to drain off some of the liquid/ moisture.

---

* Raw dairy products may contain dangerous bacteria.

Whipped Cream

Yield: *2 cups*

There is nothing that tops a yummy dessert better than a thick, creamy, deliciously sweet homemade whipped cream. It's so yummy, sometimes I just eat it by itself, but it is the perfect pairing for pie, ice cream Sundays, or a steaming cup of hot chocolate.

Ingredients

1 cup raw* or pasteurized cream

1–3 tablespoons maple syrup

1–3 teaspoons vanilla extract

Instructions

1. Pour cream, maple syrup, and vanilla into the bowl of an electric stand mixer or into another medium to large-sized bowl.
2. Either using a stand mixer fitted with whisk attachment or a hand mixer, whisk on low to medium speed until the cream forms soft peaks. You can also whisk by hand, but it will take much longer. I like to taste test along the way and adjust flavor as needed.

NOTE

Add in maple syrup and vanilla extract based on your preferred level of sweetness. I like my whipped cream sweet, so I typically add 3 tablespoons of maple syrup and 3 teaspoons of vanilla extract.

---

* Raw dairy products may contain dangerous bacteria.

Vanilla Ice Cream

Yield: *8 cups or 2 quarts*

Growing up in the Midwest, I was blessed with access to some of the best ice cream on planet Earth, so it makes sense that ice cream is probably my favorite dessert, whether by itself or on top of a brownie or slice of apple pie! Well, after testing lots of different recipes and ratios of ingredients, I can confidently say I have created the most amazing ice cream recipe!

Ingredients

3 cups raw* or pasteurized cream

½ cup raw* or pasteurized milk

6 egg yolks

¾ cup pure maple syrup

4 teaspoons vanilla extract

Instructions

1. In a large blender, add all ingredients and blend just until combined. Don't over blend, as you don't want to create a frothy consistency. I typically do about 4 pulses in my blender.
2. Pour into whichever ice cream maker you have and follow instructions of that particular ice cream maker.
3. Store in a freezer safe container with tightly sealed lid.

NOTES

If you do not have an ice cream maker, you can pour the mixture into a freezer-safe container and place in the freezer. Once placed in freezer, I like to gently stir about every 2–3 hours. I have found this creates a creamier consistency. I typically leave ice cream in the freezer for 24 hours before serving.

Raw eggs may contain salmonella and could make you sick.

---

* Raw dairy products may contain dangerous bacteria.

Chocolate Ice Cream

Yield: *8 cups or 2 quarts*

If you're a chocolate fan, try this variation on my original ice cream recipe. With this recipe I love to chop up little peanut butter cups and add them on top. There is just something magical about chocolate ice cream with peanut butter in any form.

Ingredients

3 cups raw* or pasteurized cream

½ cup raw* or pasteurized milk

6 egg yolks

¾ cup pure maple syrup

4 teaspoons vanilla extract

½ cup unsweetened cocoa

Instructions

1. In a large blender, add all ingredients and blend just until combined. Don't over blend, as you don't want to create a frothy consistency. I typically do about 4 pulses in my blender.
2. Pour into whichever ice cream maker you have and follow instructions of that particular ice cream maker.
3. Store in a freezer-safe container with a tightly sealed lid.

NOTES

If you do not have an ice cream maker, you can place into a freezer-safe container and place in freezer. Once placed in freezer, I like to gently stir about every 2–3 hours. I have found this creates a creamier consistency. I typically leave ice cream in the freezer for 24 hours before serving.

Raw eggs may contain salmonella and could make you sick.

* Raw dairy products may contain dangerous bacteria.

Sour Cream

Yield: *about 1 cup*

Sour cream is another one of those staples that is so versatile and that I always have on hand. I bet making homemade sour cream is much simpler than you expect and it's made with only three ingredients. This recipe makes a little over one cup, so double recipe if needed.

Ingredients

1 cup raw cream* (or heavy whipping cream)

2 teaspoons lemon juice or vinegar

¼ cup raw milk* (or pasteurized whole milk)

Instructions

1. In a large jar, stir together cream and lemon juice or vinegar, then stir in milk. (I like to use a large mason jar.)
2. Cover with cheesecloth and leave on counter for 24 hours.
3. Store in a sealed jar or container in refrigerator.

NOTE

Homemade sour cream will be a thinner consistency than traditional store-bought sour cream. To fix this, I like to whip my cream to almost whipped cream consistency before adding in lemon juice or vinegar and milk. This step is not necessary, but I recommend it.

---

* Raw dairy products may contain dangerous bacteria.

Cream Cheese

Yield: *about 2 cups*

Cream cheese is one of those staples that I use all the time! Pasta dishes, desserts, soups, breakfast—the list could go on forever. The cool thing about homemade cream cheese is it's only made with three ingredients that you probably already have in your fridge and pantry and it is much healthier than store-bought cream cheese because it's free of all of the gums, stabilizers, and preservatives.

Ingredients

2 cups raw milk* (pasteurized whole milk also works, but not ultra-pasteurized)

2 cups raw or pasteurized cream

2–3 tablespoons lemon juice or vinegar (I prefer lemon juice)

Salt to taste (start with ½ teaspoon)

Instructions

1. In a stainless-steel saucepan, bring milk and cream to a boil over medium heat for about 8–10 minutes. Instant thermometer should read 190°F.
2. Remove from heat and add in lemon juice or vinegar. Gently stir until combined and let sit at room temperature for 1 hour while curds form and separate from the whey.
3. Lightly wet and squeeze excess water out of your finely woven cheesecloth. Lay cheesecloth in a fine mesh strainer and place over a large bowl.
4. Pour curds into cheesecloth and let drain until whey no longer drips into the bowl (make sure bottom of the strainer does not touch the liquid in the bowl). This step should take about 30 minutes. Discard whey or save for another use.
5. Gather the sides of the cheesecloth and tie off with a string or rubber band. Suspend over empty bowl and let sit in the refrigerator until no whey drips from cheesecloth (about 2 hours).
6. Transfer cream cheese to a new bowl and add in salt. (This is also the time to add in any other seasoning or flavors you would like, such as garlic, herbs, chives, fruit, etc.) Mix well until you have a creamy consistency. You could also place in a food processor for a light, airy, and whipped consistency.
7. Store in refrigerator in an airtight container and enjoy. (Typically lasts for 7 days.)

---

* Raw dairy products may contain dangerous bacteria.

Homemade Buttermilk Ranch

Yield: *1½–2 cups*

Do we really need to say anything about ranch? It's ranch! That's enough said!

Ingredients

½ cup mayonnaise

½ cup sour cream

½ cup buttermilk or regular milk

1 tablespoon finely chopped fresh dill

½ teaspoon dried parsley

1 teaspoon finely chopped chives

½ teaspoon onion powder

½ teaspoon garlic powder

½ teaspoon salt, plus more to taste

½ teaspoon black pepper, plus more to taste

2 teaspoons lemon juice

Instructions

1. Thoroughly whisk together mayonnaise, sour cream, and buttermilk/milk.
2. Whisk in dried herbs, then add lemon juice and whisk.
3. Store refrigerated in tightly sealed jar.

CHAPTER 3

Breakfast

Sourdough Cinnamon Rolls with Icing

Yield: *6 rolls*

My sourdough cinnamon rolls are one of the most requested recipes in our house, maybe second to my biscuits and gravy. These cinnamon rolls are loved by all. They are the perfect balance of soft and fluffy with a little bit of crunch, and the citrus note in the frosting is the secret weapon in enhancing the sweet flavors without it becoming too sweet. When people tell you it's better than Cinnabon, you know you have a winner. If you really want to take these cinnamon rolls to the next level, pour about ¼ cup heavy cream over the cinnamon rolls before placing them in the oven. They come out so moist and delicious.

Note: *You can omit the orange zest and juice, but the flavor and acidity really balance the sweetness of the glaze and dough perfectly.*

Ingredients

DOUGH

⅔ cup milk

8 tablespoons unsalted butter, melted

1 egg

100 grams (½ cup) active sourdough starter

4 tablespoons sugar

360 grams (3 cups) unbleached all-purpose flour

1 teaspoon sea salt

CINNAMON-SUGAR FILLING

6 tablespoons unsalted butter, melted

½ cup sugar

4 teaspoons cinnamon

1 tablespoon flour

(Continued on next page)

Instructions

NIGHT BEFORE:

1. In a small bowl, combine milk and melted butter (make sure mixture is cool before using).
2. In the bowl of a stand mixer fitted with paddle attachment, combine egg, sourdough starter, and sugar and mix well. While it's mixing, slowly add in butter and milk mixture.
3. Add in flour and salt and continue mixing until roughly combined. It should form a sticky, shaggy dough. Scrape down the sides of the bowl, cover with a wet towel, and let rest for 30 minutes.
4. After 20 minutes, fit stand mixer with a dough hook and mix on low speed (#2 on a KitchenAid mixer) for 8 minutes. The dough should be very soft and supple and pull away from the sides of the bowl. If dough is sticky, add a little more flour.
5. Transfer dough to a well-buttered bowl, cover with plastic wrap, and let rise overnight for 12 hours.

NEXT MORNING:

1. Line a medium (9-inch) cast iron pan with parchment paper (you can also use a 9-inch spingform pan or any 9-inch baking pan/dish with high sides). If you crinkle up the parchment paper into a ball and then flatten it out, it fits into the pan more easily.

(Continued on next page)

47

GLAZE

2 tablespoons unsalted butter, softened

⅓ cup cream cheese, room temperature (see page 41)

½ cup powdered sugar, sifted

1 teaspoon vanilla

½–1 teaspoon grated orange zest

1 tablespoon milk

1 teaspoon fresh-squeezed orange juice

2. Lightly flour your work surface, gently turn out the dough onto your countertop, and pat into a rectangle. Rest for 10 minutes.

3. Dust your rolling pin in flour and roll your dough into a 16 × 12 rectangle.

4. To make the Cinnamon-Sugar Filling, in a small bowl, melt butter, then add in sugar, cinnamon, and flour to make a paste-like mixture.

5. Spread evenly across dough, leaving a ½-inch border around the edges.

6. Starting on the long edge of the dough, gently roll into a log. Be sure you are creating a tight roll so the cinnamon rolls keep shape during cutting and baking.

7. Using an oiled knife or bench scraper, cut into 6 even sections, about 2 inches each.

8. Place rolls into parchment-lined pan and let rest 1–2 hours.

9. During the second rise, preheat oven to 350°F.

10. Place rolls on center rack and bake 35–40 minutes or until golden brown.

11. While rolls are baking, make the Glaze. Whisk together softened butter, cream cheese, and sifted powdered sugar until smooth. Add in vanilla, orange zest, and milk and whisk. Slowly add in orange juice while whisking.

12. Once rolls are done, pull them out of oven and let cool 5–8 minutes. Then spread the Glaze over warm rolls and serve.

Sourdough Donuts

Yield: *12 donuts*

I have never been a huge fan of donuts, even as a little kid. I've always been more of a muffin or bread kind of girl. That was until I started making sourdough donuts from scratch, and oh my goodness, these bad boys are delicious! They're worth every minute of the time it takes to make them.

Ingredients

8 tablespoons unsalted butter, melted

⅔ cup milk

1 egg

100 grams (½ cup) active sourdough starter

4 tablespoons sugar

360 grams (3 cups) unbleached all-purpose flour

1 teaspoon sea salt

Oil or lard for frying*

Instructions

NIGHT BEFORE:

1. In a small bowl, combine melted butter and milk and allow to cool.
2. In the bowl of a stand mixer fitted with paddle attachment, combine egg, sourdough starter, and sugar and mix well. While it's mixing, slowly add in butter and milk mixture.
3. Add in flour and salt and continue mixing until roughly combined. It should form a sticky, shaggy dough. Scrape down the side of the bowl, cover with a wet towel, and let rest for 30 minutes.
4. After 20 minutes, fit stand mixer with dough hook and mix on low speed (#2 on a KitchenAid mixer) for 8 minutes. The dough should be very soft and supple and pull away from the sides of the bowl. If the dough is sticky, add a little more flour.
5. Transfer dough to a well-buttered bowl, cover with plastic wrap, and let rise overnight for 12 hours.

NEXT MORNING:

1. Lightly flour your work surface, gently turn out the dough onto your countertop, and pat into a rectangle. Rest for 10 minutes.
2. Dust rolling pin with flour and gently roll out dough to 1–2-inch thickness.

---

* I prefer to use unflavored coconut oil or lard, but you can use any oil.

(Continued on next page)

3. Using a large cookie cutter or wide-mouth mason jar, stamp out the donut rounds. (You can either leave them like this or press out the traditional donut hole in the center. If you don't have a round cutter, you can also just cut dough into small chunks and roll into small dough balls to make donut holes. Honestly, you can shape them anyway you want—don't overthink this part.)
4. Place donuts on parchment paper and let rise for 1–2 hours.
5. In a deep skillet, bring your choice of oil to proper frying temperature. Keep in mind all oils have different temperature requirements. Coconut oil should be 350°F and lard should be 350–365°F.
6. Once brought to temperature, place 3–5 donuts in the oil at a time (don't overcrowd). Fry on one side for 3–5 minutes or until golden brown, then flip over and fry for another 3–5 minutes. Then transfer to a cooling rack placed on a baking sheet or a baking sheet lined with paper towels.
7. Once cooled, top as desired. My favorite toppings are cinnamon sugar, melted chocolate, or a glaze.

NOTES

Below are a few options for toppings.

1. **Cinnamon Sugar:** *In a small bowl, mix together 1 cup sugar and 1 tablespoon cinnamon.*
2. **Melted Chocolate:** *In a microwave safe bowl, melt 1 cup chocolate chips with 1 tablespoon coconut oil. Microwave in 45-second intervals, stirring in between.*
3. **Glaze:** *Whisk together 1 cup powdered sugar with 1–3 tablespoons milk (add milk slowly until you reach desired consistency of a glaze). Add in 1–2 teaspoons vanilla to desired sweetness.*

Sourdough Pancakes

Yield: *about 10–12 (6-inch) pancakes*

As someone who is not a huge pancake lover, this is my favorite pancake recipe. I like a little crisp to the outside of my pancakes, but a soft, fluffy center. The melted butter is the trick to achieving this texture and the vanilla and cinnamon elevate the flavor of the traditionally bland pancake.

Ingredients

DRY INGREDIENTS

200 grams (1¾ cups) unbleached all-purpose flour

4 tablespoons sugar

½ teaspoon salt

1 teaspoon cinnamon

2 teaspoons baking powder

1 teaspoon baking soda

WET INGREDIENTS

200 grams (1 cup) active sourdough starter

2 eggs

1 cup milk

3 tablespoons unsalted butter, melted (plus more for cooking)

2 teaspoons vanilla

Instructions

NIGHT BEFORE:

1. In a medium bowl, whisk together dry ingredients, *except* baking powder and baking soda.
2. In a separate medium bowl, combine all wet ingredients.
3. Add wet ingredients to dry, whisk well, cover, and place in fridge overnight.

MORNING:

1. Sprinkle in baking powder and baking soda and whisk in.
2. If batter is too thick, add in a little milk 1 tablespoon at a time until you reach desired consistency.
3. On medium-low heat, melt a little butter, swirling around to coat skillet. Pour about ⅓ cup of batter into skillet. Cook 1–3 minutes or until top is full of bubbles, then carefully flip and cook another 1–3 minutes. Place on platter and loosely cover to keep warm.
4. Repeat with remaining batter, adding more butter as needed.
5. Serve with warm maple syrup, homemade whipped cream, fresh fruit, or any other topping you like!

Sourdough Waffles

Yield: *12 waffles*

I love a sweet, rich Belgian-style waffle and that is exactly what this recipe is. I like to serve with warm maple syrup, fresh fruit, and whipped cream. I love to make the batter the night before; not only does it save on time in the morning, but it helps the flavor really develop.

Ingredients

240 grams (2 cups) unbleached all-purpose flour

4 teaspoons sugar

1 teaspoon sea salt

1 teaspoon baking soda

1 cup buttermilk

6 tablespoons unsalted butter, melted

200 grams (1 cup) active sourdough starter

2 eggs

2 teaspoons cinnamon

2 teaspoons vanilla

Instructions

SAME DAY OPTION:

1. Preheat waffle maker.
2. In a large bowl, whisk together flour, sugar, salt, and baking soda and set aside.
3. In a medium bowl, whisk together buttermilk, melted butter, sourdough starter, eggs, cinnamon, and vanilla.
4. Pour wet ingredients into dry ingredients and whisk together until fully mixed. The batter should be somewhat thick but still spreadable on the waffle iron.
5. Right before you pour the batter into your waffle maker, rub a little butter on the top and bottom. Alternately, spray a little cooking spray.
6. Follow cooking times and directions for your waffle maker and *enjoy!*

OVERNIGHT OPTION:

1. In a large bowl, whisk together flour, sugar, buttermilk, melted butter, sourdough starter, cinnamon, and vanilla. Cover and place in refrigerator overnight.
2. In the morning, preheat your waffle maker.
3. Remove batter from refrigerator. In a separate bowl, whisk the eggs and pour them into the batter. Then add in salt and baking soda. Gently whisk to incorporate.
4. Right before you pour the batter into your waffle maker, rub a little butter on the top and bottom. Alternately, spray a little cooking spray.
5. Follow cooking times and directions for your waffle maker.

Sausage Gravy

Yield: *4–6 servings*

I like to think of myself as a biscuits and gravy aficionado. It is my favorite breakfast dish, so when I say I've eaten a lot of biscuits and gravy over my thirty years, I mean it. I may be biased, but this is hands down the most delicious sausage gravy you will ever try!

Ingredients

2 pounds ground breakfast sausage

4 tablespoons butter

¼ cup all-purpose flour

2 cups heavy cream

Salt to taste

Pepper to taste

½ cup milk (or less for thinning the gravy)

Instructions

1. In a large skillet, brown 2 pounds breakfast sausage over medium-high heat. Once sausage is cooked, remove from heat and pour into bowl lined with paper towel.
2. Return skillet to medium heat, melt butter, and add in flour. Whisk together and cook for 3–4 minutes to let the roux develop and cook out the flour flavor. Should have a golden color.
3. Slowly add in heavy cream and whisk. Season with salt and pepper.
4. Add the cooked sausage back in and whisk together.
5. Once brought to a boil, lower to low-medium heat and allow to simmer for 5–8 minutes. If gravy becomes too thick, you can add in a little milk to thin gravy to desired consistency.
6. Continue seasoning with salt and pepper to desired taste. I typically add quite a bit of pepper; I like the gravy to have a little bit of spice.
7. Serve with warm buttermilk biscuits (page 58) and enjoy!

Buttermilk Biscuits

Yield: *12 biscuits*

Of course, these warm, buttery biscuits are the perfect vessel for the sausage gravy, but they are equally as delicious topped with jam or honey or made into a breakfast sandwich. Or simply served on their own with some butter. They are sure to be a crowd favorite in your house.

Ingredients

2½ cups all-purpose flour

1 teaspoon salt

2 tablespoons baking powder

½ cup cold butter (cut into small chunks)

1 cup buttermilk

Instructions

1. Preheat oven to 425°F.
2. In a large bowl, whisk together flour, salt, and baking powder.
3. Add in cold butter and cut in with a pastry cutter (if you don't have a pastry cutter, you can use a fork or freeze your butter and grate it with a cheese grater).
4. Once butter is cut into pea-sized pieces, create a well in the flour and add in buttermilk. Stir until incorporated. Once you have a shaggy dough, turn out onto a lightly floured surface.
5. Work the dough until it comes together, then press into a rectangle about ½-inch thick.
6. Fold the dough over itself into thirds and press into a ½-inch thick rectangle again. Repeat this process one more time, then press into a ¾-inch thick rectangle.
7. Using a 2½-inch round biscuit cutter (you can use anything round; a wide mouth mason jar works, too), press into the dough to cut your biscuit shape.
8. Lightly grease a large cast iron pan or line a baking sheet with parchment paper and transfer biscuits to pan. Brush with buttermilk.
9. Bake biscuits for 15–20 minutes or until golden brown. Once done, brush with melted butter, allow to cool 5–10 minutes, and enjoy!

Homemade Toaster Pastries

Yield: *8 toaster pastries*

One of my go-to snacks as a kid was a Pop Tart®. They were pretty much a school lunch staple for me. Now, as an adult, I do not love the ingredients that are in a traditional store-bought toaster pastry, so this is my take on a childhood favorite, but made with real ingredients. I have included the recipes for my three favorite fillings, but you can use whatever fillings you love. Strawberry, hazelnut, and blueberry are also so delicious in these toaster pastries.

Ingredients

PASTRY CRUST

2½ cups all-purpose flour

1 tablespoon sugar

1 teaspoon salt

1 cup cold butter (cut into chunks)

¼ cup cold water

1–3 eggs for brushing

CINNAMON-BROWN SUGAR FILLING

½ cup packed brown sugar

3 teaspoons cinnamon

1 tablespoon flour

CINNAMON GLAZE

½ cup powdered sugar

½ teaspoon cinnamon

½ teaspoon vanilla extract

1 tablespoon milk

RASPBERRY FILLING

1 cup homemade (page 72) or store-bought raspberry jam

Instructions

1. To make the Pastry Crust, in a bowl, combine flour, sugar, and salt. Using a pastry cutter, cut in cold butter until the mixture forms tiny clumps the size of breadcrumbs.
2. Mix in cold water 1 tablespoon at a time until the dough comes together to form a ball. You could also use a food processor for steps 1 and 2.
3. Once dough has come together into a ball, turn it out onto a floured work surface and divide into two halves. (Dividing into two halves isn't necessary, but I find it easier to roll out smaller portions).
4. Roll each half out to ¼-inch thickness.
5. Using a knife or pizza cutter, cut both halves into 4 × 6-inch squares (be sure to finish with an even number of squares).
6. Whisk up a couple eggs in a small bowl and lightly brush all of the squares with beaten egg wash. Place one half of the egg-washed squares on a baking sheet lined with parchment paper.
7. Place Filling of choice in the center. Be sure not to over-fill and leave a little border around the edge to ensure the two halves can seal.
8. With the remaining squares, poke a few holes with a fork in each square to allow ventilation while baking. Place the other half of the squares on top of the halves with filling with the egg-washed side facing down (touching the side with the filling.) Seal toaster pastries by crimping the edges with a fork. Place in fridge for 1 hour.

VANILLA GLAZE

½ cup powdered sugar

½ teaspoon vanilla

1 tablespoon milk

9. Preheat oven to 400°F.

10. Whisk up a couple more eggs and brush toaster pastries with egg wash. Bake 25–30 minutes. The crust should be golden brown.

11. Allow to cool for 3–5 minutes, then transfer to cooling rack to cool completely. Then add glaze.

NOTES

To prepare each of the fillings and glazes, simply add the ingredients of each recipe to a small bowl and whisk together. Wait for the toaster pastries to cool completely before adding the glaze on top.

Cinnamon French Toast

Yield: *6–8 servings*

I would be lying if I said I was a French toast lover. To be honest, I have never really liked French toast, but my family is a big fan. So after years of making it for them and trying different methods and recipes, I created this one, and folks, it converted me to a French toast fan. The flavors of this recipe are the real stars, and you get that soft center with a crispy outside. It is just simply delicious.

Ingredients

Butter for cooking

8–10 slices of bread of choice (I use homemade bread, but you could also use store-bought. My favorite is thick-sliced brioche.)

6 eggs

⅓ cup milk

1½ teaspoons vanilla extract

2 teaspoons cinnamon

Powdered sugar and maple syrup

Instructions

1. In a medium-sized skillet, melt butter over medium heat.
2. In a wide, shallow dish (such as a pie pan or small baking dish), whisk together eggs, milk, vanilla extract, and cinnamon.
3. Take a slice of bread and dip each side into the mixture. Ensure you fully coat each side, but don't soak too long or bread will get soggy.
4. Immediately after dipping slice in egg mixture, transfer over to your pre-heated skillet and fry each side until golden brown. I like my French toast on the crispy side, so I cook mine a little past the point of being golden brown.
5. Serve with a light dusting of powdered sugar and warm maple syrup.

Breakfast Potatoes

Yield: *6 servings*

As a girl who grew up in the Midwest, you can bet I love potatoes—especially with breakfast. My mom has been making these potatoes for as long as I can remember; they are buttery, crispy, and so flavorful, and are sure to be a hit in your house. I make them almost every Sunday for family breakfast.

Ingredients

6–8 large or 8–10 small Yukon gold potatoes

½ yellow onion

6 tablespoons butter

Salt and pepper to taste

2 teaspoons garlic powder (or to taste)

Instructions

1. Wash and dice potatoes and set aside. (I dice in about 1-inch chunks.)
2. Finely chop onions and set aside. (You can dice them bigger if you like larger pieces of onions.)
3. In a medium skillet (I like to use a cast iron skillet for this recipe), melt 2 tablespoons butter over medium-high heat and add in diced onion. Cook until soft and translucent.
4. Add in 4 tablespoons butter and diced potatoes. Toss potatoes to fully coat in butter and cook until potatoes get crispy on all sides, occasionally stirring. Then turn down heat a little and cover to soften potatoes.
5. Once potatoes are soft and tender, remove cover and season with salt, pepper, and garlic powder to taste.

Breakfast Sausage

Yield: *4–6 servings*

For most of my life I was a bacon girl, but my husband absolutely loves sausage, so I began eating it more when we got together and now it's my breakfast meat of choice. However, most options for breakfast sausage in the grocery store have lots of sugars, nitrates, and salt. That is why I started making my own sausage, and after what felt like a thousand tries, I finally created a recipe our whole family loves.

Ingredients

1 tablespoon brown sugar

1 teaspoon salt

1 teaspoon pepper

1½ teaspoons dried sage

½ teaspoon oregano

½ teaspoon garlic powder

½ teaspoon onion powder

¼ teaspoon crushed red pepper flakes

1 pound ground pork

2 tablespoons butter

Instructions

1. Whisk together all dry ingredients in a small bowl and set aside.
2. Add ground pork to a medium-sized bowl, sprinkle seasoning mix on top, and thoroughly mix. (This is where you get your hands dirty; mixing by hand is the easiest method.) Once mixed, cover with plastic wrap or lid and place in fridge for at least 15–20 minutes. (I personally like to prepare mine the night before; the longer the mixture sits, the more the flavors will develop.)
3. Melt 2 tablespoons butter in a skillet over medium heat and add in sausage. (I like to form patties, but you could also form links or make ground breakfast sausage—whatever your preference is.)
4. Cook until sausage is cooked all the way through. If you're making links or patties and notice the outsides are getting burnt before the middle is fully cooked, turn the heat down a little. Serve with your favorite breakfast items and enjoy!

Raspberry Cream Cheese Danish

Yield: *2 Danishes*

My husband loves nothing more than a sweet treat with his morning coffee and this is one of his favorites. Our favorite Danish filling is a cream cheese and raspberry filling, which I have included in the recipe, but you could use any filling you like.

Ingredients

DANISH PASTRY DOUGH

¼ cup warm water

1 packet instant or active dry yeast

¼ cup sugar, divided

1 teaspoon salt

1 egg, at room temperature

½ cup whole milk (room temperature)

2½ cups all-purpose flour

1 cup cold butter

CREAM CHEESE FILLING

1 (8-ounce) package cream cheese

½ teaspoon vanilla

1 tablespoon sugar

RASPBERRY PRESERVE FILLING

Use homemade Raspberry Preserves (page 72) or any store-bought preserve.

EGG WASH

1 egg

2 tablespoons milk or water

Instructions

1. To make the pastry dough, begin whisking together warm water, yeast, and 1 tablespoon sugar. Cover and let sit for 5 minutes until frothy to allow yeast to activate.
2. Then whisk in remaining sugar, salt, egg, and milk. Cover and set aside.
3. Thinly slice the cold butter and place in blender or food processor. Add in flour and pulse until the butter becomes crumbly and forms pea-sized clumps.
4. Pour into the wet mixture and gently fold in with a spatula until just barely combined.
5. Place mixture onto plastic wrap, wrap tightly, and place in fridge for 6+ hours. (You can leave in fridge for up to 24–48 hours if you're making far in advance.)
6. Take the dough out and place it on a well-floured surface. Press into a rectangle with your hands. Then, with a rolling pin, roll into a 14 × 7-inch rectangle. Add more flour as needed.
7. Fold dough into thirds, like you are folding a letter, turn the dough clockwise, and roll back out to 14 inches. Repeat this process two more times (total of 3 folds).
8. Wrap in plastic wrap once again and place in fridge for at least an hour.
9. While dough is chilling in the fridge, mix together the Cream Cheese Filling ingredients. Make sure fruit preserves are chilled or at room temperature. If you are using homemade preserves, make them plenty of time in advance.

(Continued on next page)

10. Remove dough from fridge and cut in half. Wrap other half and place back in fridge, as you want the butter to stay cold until baking time. On a lightly floured piece of parchment paper, roll out to a 12 × 8-inch rectangle.

11. Spread a layer of the cream cheese filling down the center, then add the raspberry preserves. I like to swirl the mixture together a little, but this step is optional. The filling should be spread about 2 inches wide.

12. Once your filling is evenly spread down the center, use a sharp knife or pizza cutter to cut strips down each side, about 1-inch wide and at an angle.

13. Fold the strips over the filling, alternating each side in a braiding pattern.

14. Repeat with the second batch of dough (unless you're freezing it to save for later).

15. Whisk up the egg wash and brush the top of the dough.

16. Place back in the fridge for 15–20 minutes (this step isn't necessary but does help the Danish bake better and not leak as much butter).

17. Preheat oven to 400°F. Bake for 20–22 minutes until golden brown.

18. Allow to cool and enjoy!

Raspberry Preserves/Jam

Yield: *½ pint*

A while back, my husband and I found this wonderful little place in Bigfork, Montana that made preserves and jams with the hundred-year-old recipes of a woman named Eva Gates. While there, I tried their raspberry preserves and it was the most amazing preserve I had ever tasted. I knew I needed to create my own amazing raspberry preserve recipe. This is it.

Ingredients

1 cup raspberries

½ cup sugar

Zest of ½ lemon

Juice of ½ lemon

Instructions

1. Thoroughly wash and dry raspberries.
2. Add raspberries to a medium saucepan with the sugar, lemon zest, and lemon juice and bring to a boil over medium-high heat. Gently mash the raspberries and stir occasionally.
3. Once at a boil, continue cooking for another 5 minutes, then turn heat to low and simmer for 10–15 minutes.
4. Remove from heat and let cool for 5–8 minutes. You will notice the preserves will start to thicken. Transfer into ½ pint jar, and once cool cover with lid and place in fridge. The preserves will continue to thicken to the consistency of traditional jam/preserves.

CHAPTER 4

Dinner

Not Your Grandma's Meatloaf

Yield: *5–6 servings*

As much as I would love to take credit for this recipe, it is all my mama. You will notice it's a bit different from a traditional meatloaf, and the combination of the ketchup and BBQ sauce is the secret ticket. You can also make this with any type of ground meat—chicken or turkey are great options, but my favorite is ground bison. Serve with mashed potatoes. I promise once you try this recipe, you will never make meatloaf any other way. I usually make the meatloaf mixture in the morning, place in a bowl, cover, and let sit in fridge until dinner time to allow all of the flavors to develop.

Ingredients

1 pound ground beef

1 egg

1 cup Italian bread crumbs

1 tablespoon Italian seasoning

1 tablespoon garlic powder

1 tablespoon onion powder or dried onion

1 tablespoon sea salt

1 tablespoon pepper

1 cup finely grated Parmesan

½ cup ketchup

½ cup BBQ sauce

Instructions

1. Preheat oven to 350°F.
2. In a medium bowl, mix together all ingredients except ketchup and BBQ sauce with your hands just until well combined. (Be careful not to over-mix.)
3. Spray a 9 × 13-inch baking dish with a little cooking spray (I prefer a glass baking dish for this recipe). Place meatloaf mixture in dish and gently form into a log-like rectangle.
4. Bake for 30 minutes. While meatloaf is baking, mix together ketchup and BBQ sauce in a small bowl.
5. Remove meatloaf from oven, pour ketchup and BBQ sauce mixture over top, covering the meatloaf completely, and return to oven for another 15–20 minutes.
6. Remove from oven and let cool for 5–10 minutes before serving.

Michelle's Famous Mashed Potatoes

Yield: *8–10 servings*

Mashed potatoes are hands down my favorite side dish. Whether for a holiday dinner or a regular Tuesday night, I could eat these with any meal, any time. The ingredient that makes this recipe so good is the use of heavy cream instead of the traditionally used milk; it gives the potatoes the creamiest, silkiest texture.

Ingredients

5 pounds potato of choice (I like to use Yukon gold)

1 cup (2 sticks) unsalted butter

½–¾ cup heavy cream

Salt and pepper to taste

Instructions

1. Wash and cut potatoes. If using Yukon golds or redskin potatoes, I like to leave the skin on. If you choose to do that, make sure you very thoroughly wash them. If using russet potatoes, I typically like to wash and peel them, as they have a tougher skin. Depending on size of potatoes, I typically cut in eighths for larger potatoes. If they are small, then I just quarter them.
2. Place in a large pot and fill with water until potatoes are completely covered. Sprinkle in a little salt and cook on high heat until potatoes are tender.
3. Once potatoes are tender, carefully strain water from potatoes. If you are using a colander, transfer potatoes back to pot after straining.
4. Before adding any ingredients, I like to give the potatoes a rough mash. I use a hand masher because it gives the best texture and consistency in my opinion, but you can use an electric mixer if that's what you prefer.
5. Cut each stick of butter into 4 cubes, add to potatoes, and give them a good mash. Then add in cream. Start with ½ cup and add more if needed to achieve desired consistency. Add in salt and pepper to taste (start with a moderate amount and add more in as you taste). Keep mashing until you achieve desired consistency. I like them smooth and creamy but with some small chunks for texture.

Pasta

Yield: *about 4 cups prepared pasta*

Up until a few years ago, I had never made homemade pasta, but once I did I knew I would never go back to store-bought again. When you try it, you will know what I mean. Many think making pasta from scratch is difficult and time-consuming, but it actually only adds about 10–15 minutes to your cooking time. Even less if you make the pasta dough ahead of time.

Ingredients

2 cups all-purpose flour, plus more for dusting

6 eggs

1 teaspoon salt, plus more for boiling pasta

Instructions

1. Place 2 cups of flour on a well-cleaned surface.
2. Create a well in the center of the flour and crack in eggs and add salt.
3. With a fork, break up the egg yolks and begin whisking the eggs, slowly incorporating flour as you whisk.
4. Once all of the flour is incorporated and whisked in with the eggs, begin kneading the pasta dough. Fold one end over the middle and press down in a forward motion, make a quarter turn, and repeat. You will keep repeating this process for about 8–10 minutes until the dough becomes soft and supple. Wrap in plastic wrap and place in fridge for 25 minutes to an hour. (You can also make ahead and take out when ready to shape and cook the pasta.)
5. Remove from fridge and place on a well-floured surface. Using a bench scraper or sharp knife, cut the dough into 4–6 sections. Take each section and roll out using a rolling pin until about ¼-inch thick.
6. For this step, you have some options:
   a. Use a rolling pin to keep rolling dough until very thin and almost translucent, then cut into individual pasta pieces. (Warning: it takes a long time to roll out this way, so be prepared.)
   b. If you have a hand-cranked pasta roller, you can use that. Just roll with rolling pin until thin enough to fit into pasta roller and proceed from there.
   c. If you have a KitchenAid stand mixer, fit with the pasta roller attachment. Place speed on high and feed rolled-out dough through attachment starting with level 8, then work down by 2 (ie: 8-6-4-2). When pasta has been rolled out, set aside and continue with the other sections of pasta dough. Once all dough is rolled out, switch attachment to the pasta cutter you prefer (mine came with a fettuccini and spaghetti-sized pasta cutter). Run your sheets of pasta dough through and hang on a spaghetti rack if you have one. Or just lay flat on a well-floured surface and continue until all pasta is cut and ready.
7. Fill up a medium-sized pot with water and generously salt (I'm talking a tablespoon or two. Fresh pasta needs a saltier water than traditional store-bought dried pasta. Bring to a boil and add in pasta.
8. Cook until pasta is cooked and tender, about 8–10 minutes. Fresh pasta cooks very quickly.
9. Drain water and serve with your favorite pasta sauce and toppings.

Alfredo Sauce

Yield: *4–6 servings*

My love of alfredo started at a young age. What is better than pasta, cream, butter, and cheese, am I right? This is a super easy recipe to throw together or make ahead. I like to top mine off with a piece of grilled chicken.

Ingredients

4 tablespoons butter

1 tablespoon fresh minced garlic
  (3–4 cloves)

2 tablespoons flour

2 cups heavy cream

2 cups milk

1 heaping cup grated Parmesan

1 heaping cup grated asiago

1 tablespoon salt

1 tablespoon black pepper

Instructions

1. In a large saucepan, melt butter over medium heat.
2. Once melted and bubbling, add in garlic and sauté until golden and aromatic (stirring occasionally).
3. Add in flour and whisk until well-combined.
4. Pour in cream and milk and whisk together.
5. Whisk in grated cheeses, salt, and pepper.
6. Once combined, lower temperature to low heat and simmer until ready to serve. Sauce should begin to thicken and have a creamy consistency. Continue whisking occasionally to prevent burning.
7. Add in cooked pasta and give it a good toss. Serve by itself or add in your favorite protein.

Marinara Sauce

Yield: *4–6 servings*

I have always been a big spaghetti lover, but as I've gotten older store-bought marinara tends to give me heartburn from the acidity. This homemade marinara, on the other hand, does not. It is a much lighter sauce, something more similar to how traditional marinara in Italian cuisine is made. What's great about this recipe is you can make large batches of it and add to your food storage. You can freeze, freeze dry, or can this recipe and have fresh homemade marinara for months or years to come.

Ingredients

2 tablespoons butter

¼ cup olive oil

2 tablespoons (8–10 cloves) fresh minced garlic

1 onion, finely chopped

2 cups finely chopped mushrooms (any variety)

3 tablespoons tomato paste

4 tablespoons dried oregano

4 tablespoons Italian seasoning

2 tablespoons sugar

1 (28-ounce) can San Marzano whole peeled tomatoes

1 (14-ounce) can San Marzano crushed tomatoes

4 tablespoons (15–20 leaves) roughly chopped fresh basil

1 teaspoon salt

Instructions

1. In a large saucepan with deep sides, add butter and olive oil over medium heat.
2. Once bubbling, add in garlic and sauté until aromatic, 3–5 minutes. Add in onion and cook until soft and translucent.
3. Add in mushrooms and sauté until soft and tender, then add in tomato paste and give the mixture a good stir. Add in oregano, Italian seasoning, and sugar and stir.
4. Add in can of crushed tomatoes. Hand-crush the whole tomatoes by squeezing each tomato in your hand, and then add to pan. Add remaining juice from cans and stir.
5. Add in fresh basil and turn down to low heat to simmer.
6. Add salt to taste. The key to great sauces is flavoring to taste. Once sauce has simmered for 15–20 minutes, give it a taste and add more seasonings where needed.
7. Allow sauce to simmer, stirring occasionally for 30–40 minutes minimum. The longer you can simmer your sauce, the more the flavors will develop.
8. Serve on top of your favorite pasta, use as a pizza sauce, or can/freeze for later use.

Chicken Pot Pie

Yield: *8 servings*

Is there anything more comforting than a delicious hearty chicken pot pie? If I am craving something warm and savory, this is what I make. My favorite way to serve this dish is a heaping scoop overtop mashed potatoes.

Ingredients

FILLING

3 bone-in skin-on chicken breasts
   (or a rotisserie chicken, meat cut off)

Salt and pepper to taste

1 sprinkle Italian seasoning

4 tablespoons butter

⅓ cup finely chopped onion

½ cup finely diced carrot

⅓ cup finely chopped celery

⅓ cup all-purpose flour

2 cups chicken bone broth

Chopped fresh thyme to taste

½ cup heavy cream

⅓ cup peas (optional)

1 egg

1 tablespoon water

CRUST

1½ cups all-purpose flour

½ teaspoon salt

8 tablespoons (½ cup) cold unsalted butter

¼ cup ice water

Instructions

1. Preheat oven to 375°F. Place chicken breasts in baking dish and season generously with salt, pepper, and a sprinkle of Italian seasoning. Bake for 45 minutes. When done baking, allow to cool, then shred the chicken. (You can skip this step if you are using a store-bought rotisserie chicken. Just shred 3 cups worth of the chicken.)

2. Prepare the crust dough. In a medium bowl, add flour and salt. Cut butter in with a pastry cutter or fork until the mixture is crumbly and butter is pea-sized.

3. Add in ice water 1 tablespoon at a time, mixing it in with a fork. You may not need all of the water and be careful not to over-mix. Once combined, mold into a ball and gently press the dough with your hand to flatten into a disc shape. Wrap in plastic wrap and place in fridge while you prepare the filling.

4. If you are using a prepared rotisserie chicken, now is when you preheat oven to 375°F.

5. In a large saucepan over medium heat, melt butter and add onions, carrots, and celery. Stir until onions start to become translucent, about 3–5 minutes. Add in flour and stir to combine. Cook for a couple minutes then add in bone broth. Give it a good stir and let it cook and thicken.

6. Once filling becomes thickened, add in chicken, salt, pepper, and thyme. Keep tasting filling throughout cooking and adjust seasoning as needed.

7. Add in cream and stir. Turn the heat to low and let simmer, stirring occasionally. If you are incorporating peas (frozen or fresh), now is when you will add them. If filling becomes too thick, you can add in a little more bone

broth. Simmer for about 5–10 more minutes and then remove from heat to allow it to cool a bit.

8. Remove pie crust from fridge, place a damp cloth on your counter, and place a piece of parchment paper on top. Lightly flour the parchment paper and place the pie crust on it. Roll out the pie crust into a circle or whatever shape your baking dish is (I recommend a 2-quart baking dish). Always start rolling from the center and work outward, alternating all directions.

9. Pour filling into baking dish and carefully transfer pie crust to top of dish. Pinch the crust to the side of the baking dish to create a seal, then cut a few slits in the top to allow for ventilation.

10. Whisk up egg and water to make the egg wash. Brush the egg wash all over the top of the crust.

11. Bake for 25–30 minutes, until the crust is a deep golden brown.

12. Allow to cool for about 5–8 minutes to help the dish set up, then serve.

Grilled Cheese Sandwich & Tomato Soup

Yield: *8–12 servings*

Grilled cheese and tomato soup is one of those meals I crave when the seasons are cooler. This is an elevated version of a simple, classic comfort meal. Who doesn't love a gooey grilled cheese on a buttery toasted sourdough bread, dipped in a rich, hearty tomato soup?

Ingredients

TOMATO SOUP

6 medium tomatoes

5 large carrots

1 large red onion

6 cloves garlic

2 tablespoons olive oil

2 cups bone broth (homemade, page 120, or store-bought) or vegetable broth

2 handfuls fresh basil, divided

1 cup heavy cream

1 teaspoon sea salt, plus more for taste

Black pepper to taste

GRILLED CHEESE SANDWICH

2 slices bread (I use homemade sourdough bread)

2 thin slices white cheddar

2 thin slices sharp cheddar cheese

2 tablespoons butter

Instructions

1. Preheat oven to 375°F.
2. Wash and quarter tomatoes, carrots, and onion and place on a large sheet pan. Peel garlic and add to sheet pan. Drizzle with olive oil and thoroughly mix so everything is evenly coated in olive oil.
3. Bake for 30–40 minutes. Everything should be very tender and almost caramelized.
4. Carefully remove from oven and let cool for 10–15 minutes, then transfer to a Dutch oven or large pot.
5. Over medium heat, pour in bone broth or vegetable broth and add a handful of basil. Blend with an immersion blender until smooth or place in a blender and blend until smooth before adding into Dutch oven.
6. Add in cream, salt, and pepper. Roughly tear a hand full of basil and add to pot. Bring to a boil, then drop heat to low and let simmer, occasionally stirring.
7. After 10–15 minutes, taste and add more salt, pepper, and basil as needed. Simmer for another 15–20 minutes or longer. The longer the soup simmers, the more the flavors will develop.
8. While soup is simmering, place a medium skillet on high-medium heat and melt 1 tablespoon of butter in it. Once melted, lay down the first piece of bread and swirl around to completely cover side with butter. Place slices of cheese on bread and add top piece of bread.
9. Let cook for 5–8 minutes until bottom piece of bread is dark golden brown and crispy.
10. Using a spatula, lift up sandwich, add another 1 tablespoon of butter to the pan, let melt, and then flip grilled cheese over and place back in skillet. Cook until golden brown and crispy.
11. Serve with a delicious bowl of tomato soup.

Sourdough Fried Chicken

Yield: *4–6 servings*

This is one of the most flavorful fried chicken recipes I have ever created. The buttermilk and sourdough dredges are the two key ingredients that take this fried chicken to the next level. I know using sourdough starter in a fried chicken recipe might sound odd, but trust me, it is amazing.

Note: *I prefer to use rendered lard or unflavored coconut oil, but any frying oil will work.*

Ingredients

100 grams (½ cup) sourdough starter discard

1 cup buttermilk

4 tablespoons salt, divided

4 tablespoons black pepper, divided

4 tablespoons garlic powder, divided

4 teaspoons cayenne powder, divided

2 cups all-purpose flour

1 pound boneless skinless chicken breast, split in half

Oil for frying (about 10 cups; see notes)

Instructions

1. In a bowl, whisk together sourdough starter discard, buttermilk, 2 tablespoons each of salt, pepper, garlic powder, and 2 teaspoons cayenne powder. Set aside.
2. Pat dry and lightly season chicken breasts with salt and pepper.
3. Divide flour evenly into 2 bowls. Add other 2 tablespoons each of salt, black pepper, garlic powder, and 2 teaspoons of cayenne powder to one of the bowls of flour and whisk until combined.
4. In a deep skillet or pot, pour in oil (should be about 4 inches deep). Heat on medium-high heat until you reach 350°F (attach frying or candy thermometer to pot to check temperature).
5. Dredge chicken in unseasoned flour and shake off access. Then dip into sourdough stater discard batter, then dredge into seasoned flour, and then place into the frying oil. Add in 3–4 pieces of chicken at a time. Don't over-crowd pan. Temperature will drop when you add the chicken, so adjust the heat as necessary to maintain 330°F to 350°F.
6. Fry chicken until dark golden brown, about 10 minutes. Transfer to wire cooling rack with baking sheet underneath and allow to drain and cool (about 5 minutes).
7. Transfer to platter and serve.

Big Gooey Messy Burger

Yield: *4 servings*

To quote my favorite childhood movie, I had to call this delicious recipe the Big Gooey Messy Burger, but it is also known as a sloppy joe. After making this recipe, it's hard to go back to store-bought sloppy joe mix, and that's the whole point. This recipe is so flavorful and, in my opinion, the way a sloppy joe should taste. The flavors are fresh and bright and it's so easy to throw together on a busy weeknight. I like to double this recipe for leftovers.

Ingredients

2 tablespoons butter

½ yellow onion, chopped

½ red bell pepper, seeded and finely diced

½ green bell pepper, seeded and finely diced

1 pound ground beef

1 tablespoon tomato paste

½ cup ketchup

2 tablespoons yellow mustard (more for taste)

1 tablespoon brown sugar

1 teaspoon salt, or to taste

½ teaspoon black pepper, or to taste

½ teaspoon garlic powder

4 hamburger buns

Instructions

1. In a medium saucepan over medium heat, melt 2 tablespoons butter. Add in chopped onion and diced peppers. Stir and sauté until softened, about 8 minutes.
2. Add in ground beef and brown until cooked thoroughly.
3. Add in tomato paste and stir to combine. Add in ketchup, mustard, and brown sugar. Stir to combine.
4. Season with salt, pepper, and garlic. Stir.
5. Reduce heat to medium-low and allow to cook for 15–20 minutes.
6. Enjoy piled high on a hamburger bun.

Dad's Famous Chili

Yield: *8 servings*

During football season, this dish is always on repeat. I love a warm bowl of chili on a cool fall day. The recipe is the perfect marriage of heartiness, a little spice, and a lightness when most chili is very dense. I have learned that when it comes to chili, there is no one right way to make it and everyone's palate is different, so take this recipe and adjust the spices and seasonings to fit your liking.

Ingredients

1 pound ground beef

1 pound spicy ground Italian sausage

1 medium onion, diced

1 jalapeño, seeded diced

1 green bell pepper, seeded and diced

2 tablespoons chili powder, or to taste

1–2 teaspoons salt, or to taste

1–2 teaspoons pepper, or to taste

1–3 teaspoons garlic powder, or to taste

28-ounce can whole tomatoes with juice

15-ounce can tomato sauce

2 (15-ounce) cans chili beans (pinto beans with chili sauce)

15-ounce can dark red kidney beans, rinsed and drained

Cheddar cheese, grated, for serving

Sour cream, for serving

Tortilla chips, for serving

Instructions

1. In a large deep pot over medium-high heat, brown ground beef and Italian sausage. Once cooked, add in onion, jalapeño, and bell pepper and stir. Season with chili powder, salt, pepper, and garlic powder. Stir.
2. Add whole tomatoes, tomato sauce, and beans into pot. Bring to a boil, then reduce heat to low and let simmer 4–6 hours or longer. Stir occasionally to prevent burning at the bottom and taste every so often, adjusting seasoning as necessary.
3. Serve with cheese, sour cream, and tortilla chips.

Baked Potato Soup

Yield: *8 servings*

There is something so comforting about a big hearty bowl of baked potato soup. I make this at least a couple times a month in the winter season. I recommend using the bone broth in this recipe because it adds another layer of nutrients, which is especially important in those cold winter months.

Ingredients

3 tablespoons butter

1 sweet onion, finely diced

3–4 cloves minced garlic

4 whole carrots, diced

5–7 russet potatoes, peeled and diced

1 teaspoon salt, or to taste

1 teaspoon black pepper, or to taste

3 tablespoons flour

4 cups bone broth (homemade, page 120, or store-bought) or vegetable broth

2 cups heavy cream

2 cups freshly grated cheddar cheese, plus more for topping, optional

Bacon, chopped, for topping, optional

Chives, chopped, for topping, optional

Instructions

1. In a deep pot or Dutch oven over medium heat, melt butter and sauté onions until softened, then add in minced garlic. Cook for a few minutes until onions are translucent and garlic is aromatic, then add in carrots. Continue cooking for about 3–5 minutes, stirring occasionally

2. Add potatoes and season with salt and pepper. Cook for 5–10 minutes. Stir in flour and cook for a few minutes to remove raw flour taste.

3. Stir in bone broth and bring to a boil. Once at a boil, cook for about 10 minutes, then slightly lower heat.

4. Stir in heavy cream.

5. Stir in grated cheese and allow to melt completely, stirring occasionally. Add more salt and pepper to taste.

6. Allow to simmer over low heat for at least 2–3 hours.

7. Serve with your favorite toppings. I like to top with a little more grated cheddar, chopped bacon, and freshly chopped chives.

Pot Roast

Yield: *6–8 servings*

Nothing tastes like home or childhood more than a delicious hearty pot roast. This is a meal I remember my grandma making frequently. My family is from the rural Midwest where this is a staple, especially in the colder months because it's made from ingredients that preserve well from the harvest that year. What's more Midwest than meat and potatoes?

Ingredients

1 onion

2 pounds yellow potatoes

6 carrots

2–3 pounds chuck roast

1 tablespoon salt

1 tablespoon pepper

1 tablespoon garlic powder

2 tablespoons butter

2 bay leaves

3–4 sprigs of fresh thyme

2 cups beef bone broth

GRAVY

2 tablespoons butter, melted

2 tablespoons flour

2 cups drippings from cooked pot roast

½–1 teaspoon salt, or to taste

½–1 teaspoon garlic powder, or to taste

½–1 teaspoon onion powder, or to taste

Instructions

1. Preheat oven to 300°F and give onion, potatoes, and carrots a rough chop. Set aside.
2. Season chuck roast with salt, pepper, and garlic powder.
3. On high heat in your dutch oven, melt butter and sear each side of chuck roast. Be careful, butter and drippings from roast tend to splatter.
4. Once seared, add in onion, potatoes, carrots, bay leaves, and sprigs of thyme. Pour in bone broth. Cover and place in oven to cook for 2–3 hours, until the potatoes are fork-tender and the roast easily pulls apart.

FOR THE GRAVY:

1. In a small pot over medium heat, whisk together melted butter and flour to make a roux. Cook for 2–3 minutes.
2. Remove 2 cups of the cooked pot roast juices/drippings and whisk into the roux. Season with salt, pepper, garlic powder, and onion powder to taste. Bring to a boil, then lower heat and simmer until gravy begins to thicken.

Beef Stroganoff

Yield: *6 servings*

This is a recipe I created by accident recently. I didn't have dinner planned and was just throwing things I had on hand together. When I took that first bite, I knew it had to go in the book. This is one of those meals that will make you sigh after taking a bite because it's that good. I love to serve this with warm bread and butter.

Ingredients

- 1 (16-ounce) package of wide egg noodles or homemade wide noodles (see page 81 for recipe, but cut noodles wider)
- 4 tablespoons butter, divided
- 1 pound thinly sliced steak (or shredded beef or meatballs)
- 1 medium yellow onion, finely chopped
- 4 cloves garlic, minced
- 2 cups sliced mushrooms, such as baby bellas
- 3 tablespoons flour
- 2 cups beef bone broth
- 2 tablespoons Worcestershire sauce
- ½ cup sour cream
- ½ cup heavy cream
- 1 cup freshly grated Parmesan
- Salt and pepper to taste

Instructions

1. In a large pot of boiling, salted water, cook noodles until al dente, then drain water. (For best timing, add noodles to boiling water when you get to step 4.)
2. Melt 2 tablespoons butter over medium-high heat in a large skillet. Add steak in a single layer and cook for about 3 minutes, then flip steak to other side and cook another 3 minutes. Remove from pan and set aside.
3. Add 2 more tablespoons of butter to pan. Once melted, add in onions and garlic. Cook for a few minutes, then add in mushrooms, stirring occasionally.
4. Once onions are translucent, add in flour to make a roux. Stir in thoroughly.
5. Add in bone broth and Worcestershire sauce. Mix thoroughly, then let simmer for 8–10 minutes.
6. Stir in sour cream, heavy cream, and Parmesan. Season with salt and pepper to taste. Let simmer, stirring occasionally, until sauce begins to thicken. (If sauce becomes too thick, you can add a little more broth.)
7. Add in cooked steak and noodles and give a good toss to evenly coat everything with stroganoff sauce.

Homemade Meatballs

Yield: *about 20 meatballs*

A homemade meatball recipe is the perfect addition to any cooking repertoire. Meatballs are so versatile, and I am constantly finding new ways to use them: spaghetti, stroganoff, with BBQ sauce, a creamy mushroom sauce—the possibilities are truly endless. Any time I make meatballs, I make double or triple what I need for that meal, portion them out, and freeze them for future recipes.

Ingredients

2 pounds ground beef

1 cup bread crumbs

1 tablespoon Italian seasoning

2 teaspoons garlic powder

2 teaspoons pepper

2 teaspoons salt

1 cup finely grated Parmesan cheese.

2 eggs

2 tablespoons olive oil

Instructions

1. Add all ingredients except oil to a large bowl and mix well with hands. Form 2-inch balls and set aside on a baking dish.
2. In a large skillet, heat 2 tablespoons olive oil over medium heat. Place meatballs in skillet and sear each side of the meatball, about 3–4 minutes on each side.
3. If you are making with marinara, add seared meatballs to sauce, cover, and let finish cooking in sauce, about 30–35 minutes. If you are making them by themselves, turn the heat to low, cover, and let cook 30–35 minutes. Uncover the skillet and turn the meatballs frequently to prevent sides from burning.

Beef Stew

Yield: *6–8 servings*

One of my favorite meals growing up was the beef stew that came in a can. While my taste buds have been refined a bit since then, that love of beef stew is still there. This beef stew is a great dish when you are wanting a simple but comforting meal. It's one of those meals you just throw together, let it cook, then enjoy!

Ingredients

2 tablespoons butter, divided

2 tablespoons olive oil, divided

2 pounds stew meat or boneless beef chuck, cut into 1-inch pieces

1 yellow onion

6 cloves garlic

2 tablespoons Worcestershire sauce

1 tablespoon tomato paste

¼ cup all-purpose flour

2 cups red wine

3 cups beef bone broth

1 bay leaf

1 teaspoon sugar

1 pound small yellow potatoes, cut in half or quartered

5 large carrots, cut into 1-inch chunks

2 teaspoons salt

2 teaspoons pepper

Instructions

1. In a Dutch oven over medium-high heat, melt 1 tablespoon butter and 1 tablespoon olive oil. Place meat down in an even layer to sear the sides. You don't want to over-crowd the pan, so sear in batches, adding more butter and olive oil when needed. Once all meat is seared on all sides, about 5 minutes per batch, remove from pan and set aside.

2. Add remaining olive oil and butter to Dutch oven and add in onions, garlic, and Worcestershire sauce. Stir well, then add in tomato paste and cook for a few more minutes, stirring and scraping up all of the brown bits from the bottom of the Dutch oven.

3. Add meat back in and sprinkle flour over top. Stir until combined and flour is dissolved.

4. Add in wine and bone broth, bay leaf, and sugar. Stir to combine. Cover and simmer on low heat for 2 hours.

5. After 2 hours, add in potatoes and carrots. Season with salt and pepper. Cover and let simmer another hour, adjust seasonings to taste, remove bay leaf, then enjoy!

Ooey Gooey Mac & Cheese

Yield: *8 servings*

Who doesn't love an ooey gooey macaroni and cheese? This recipe is a great make-ahead dish that you can keep in the freezer until you are ready to throw it in the oven to bake. I love making this for parties or potlucks; it keeps well, it's easy to reheat, and travels easily.

Ingredients

1 box elbow noodles

7 tablespoons butter, divided

⅓ cup all-purpose flour

2 cups heavy cream

1 cup whole milk

2½ cups shredded sharp cheddar cheese

1 cup shredded Gruyère cheese

Salt and pepper to taste

Parmesan cheese, optional

Breadcrumbs, optional

Instructions

1. Boil salted water and cook pasta a few minutes less than box directions for al dente. Drain and add in 1 tablespoon butter and stir around the pasta. (Butter will prevent the pasta from sticking.)
2. In a large saucepan over medium heat, make a roux by melting 6 tablespoons of butter and whisking in flour, cooking for a minute or two once combined.
3. While continuously whisking, slowly add in heavy cream and then milk. Continue cooking over medium heat and continuously whisking until sauce becomes very thick.
4. Remove from heat and add in ⅓ of the cheese, whisking until combined and smooth. Then add in another ⅓, whisking until smooth. Add the remaining cheese and whisk until smooth. Season with salt and pepper to taste.
5. Add in cooked pasta and give it a stir. This is where I like to stop and serve it, but you could also transfer to a greased baking dish, top with Parmesan cheese and breadcrumbs, and bake at 325°F for 15–20 minutes until golden on top.

Chicken Noodle Soup

Yield: *12 servings*

This is my go-to dish when anyone in my family is feeling under the weather. This recipe has great immune-boosting ingredients such as bone broth, onions, carrots, and oregano. It also just makes the soul feel good when you eat it. I like to serve with crackers to add a little crunch to the soup.

Ingredients

3 tablespoons butter

1 medium yellow onion, diced

4 carrots, chopped

2 celery stalks, chopped

1 whole chicken

8 cups chicken bone broth or low-sodium chicken broth

1 tablespoon fresh parsley (or 1 teaspoon dried)

1 tablespoon fresh oregano (or 1 teaspoon dried)

1 tablespoon fresh thyme (or 1 teaspoon dried)

Salt and pepper to taste

2–3 cups egg noodles (for homemade, see page 81, but cut noodles wide)

Instructions

1. In a Dutch oven or large pot, melt butter over medium-high heat.
2. Add in chopped onion, carrots, and celery. Sauté for 3–5 minutes until onions are softened.
3. Place whole chicken in pot, pour in all of the bone broth, and add in all seasonings. Cover and let cook on low-medium heat for 2–3 hours or unil chicken is cooked.
4. Turn heat down to low.
5. Remove entire chicken and transfer to plate. Allow to cool for a few minutes, then remove meat from bones and shred the meat.
6. Once shredded, add chicken meat back to the soup, then add in noodles. (If using homemade noodles, cook until al dente in a separate pot of boiling salted water. If using store-bought noodles, just add them right into the soup uncooked).
7. Continue cooking on low until noodles are soft and tender. Taste and add more seasonings as desired.

Lasagna

Yield: *8 servings*

This recipe is my unique take on a traditional lasagna. You will notice it is missing one ingredient that is almost always in lasagna—ricotta cheese. That is because I am not a huge fan of the taste or texture of ricotta, so I substitute it for cream cheese and it makes the lasagna out of this world.

Ingredients

SAUCE

1 tablespoon butter

1 tablespoon olive oil

1 finely chopped onion

2 tablespoons fresh minced garlic (8–10 cloves)

3 tablespoons tomato paste

28-ounce can San Marzano whole peeled tomatoes

14-ounce can San Marzano crushed tomatoes (or 3–4 jars home canned tomatoes in place of both cans of store-bought tomatoes)

4 tablespoons dried oregano

4 tablespoons Italian seasoning

4 tablespoons roughly chopped fresh basil (15–20 leaves)

2 tablespoons sugar

Salt to taste

PASTA

2 cups all-purpose flour

6 eggs

1 teaspoon salt

(Continued on next page)

Instructions

1. Start by making the Sauce. In a large pot over medium heat, heat butter and olive oil. Add in onion and sauté 2–3 minutes. Add in garlic and continue to sauté.
2. Once onions are translucent, add in tomato paste and give it a good stir to combine. Add in tomatoes and all seasonings. Turn to low heat and let simmer while you make the Pasta and Filling.
3. To make the Pasta, combine all the ingredients and roll out into thin sheets. Cut to fit baking dish. You will need 5–7 sheets of pasta. Cook pasta in a pot of boiling salted water until barely cooked. Pasta should be just soft enough to work with. Remove from water, brush with olive oil (to prevent sticking), and set aside.
4. To make the Filling, brown ground beef, then add in cream cheese, Parmesan, and seasonings.
5. Remove everything from heat for about 5 minutes to cool a little, then grab a glass baking dish. Any size you have will work (just cut pasta to fit dish).
6. Preheat oven to 350°F.
7. Lightly butter the dish, then begin by adding a little sauce to the bottom.
8. Lay down a sheet of Pasta, add ground beef Filling, then smother in Sauce and evenly spread some mozzarella on top.
9. Add another layer of Pasta and repeat process until you reach the top of your baking dish. On top of the last layer of Sauce, add a good amount of mozzarella and a little bit of grated Parmesan.

(Continued on next page)

FILLING

1 pound ground beef

2 (8-ounce) blocks cream cheese

1 cup freshly grated Parmesan

1 teaspoon Italian seasoning

1 teaspoon oregano

1 teaspoon salt

2 cups mozzarella

10. Place assembled lasagna in oven and bake about 15 minutes or until top is golden brown and cheese is bubbly.
11. Remove from oven and let sit 8–10 minutes to allow lasagna to set before serving.

Mama's Famous Baked Chicken

Yield: *3–4 servings*

Every time I go home to visit my mom, I request her baked chicken. It is so amazing! For this recipe, I like to use bone-in skin-on chicken breasts because the meat is so juicy and tender, but those can be hard to find so you can substitute with chicken thighs. Just make sure you are using a bone-in skin-on cut of chicken.

Ingredients

2–3 pounds (about 3–4) bone-in skin-on chicken breasts

Italian seasoning

Salt

Pepper

Instructions

1. Preheat oven to 375°F.
2. Pat chicken dry then place chicken in baking dish (I use a glass dish) and evenly season with salt, pepper, and Italian seasoning. There are no exact measurements, but give the chicken a good coat of seasoning.
3. Place in oven and bake for 45 min–1 hour until tops are golden brown and crispy. You can also check internal temperature; they should be 165°F in the center.

CHAPTER 5

Sides

Cheesy Scalloped Potatoes

Yield: *6 servings*

Scalloped potatoes are one of my favorite side dishes to make when I'm hosting a dinner or need to bring a dish to pass. Once you get the prep work done, the rest of the dish is easy to throw together.

Ingredients

2 tablespoons butter

1 small onion, diced

3 cloves garlic, minced

2 tablespoons flour

1 cup milk

½ cup heavy cream

1 teaspoon salt

1 teaspoon pepper

1 dash paprika

2 cups grated sharp cheddar cheese, divided

4 cups thinly sliced Yukon gold potatoes

½ cup grated Parmesan

Instructions

1. Preheat oven to 375°F and grease a 9 × 13-inch baking dish.
2. Using a mandolin or knife, thinly slice potatoes. Pat dry and set aside. In a large pot (I like to use my Dutch oven), melt butter over medium heat and add in diced onion. Sauté for 3–5 minutes until soft and translucent, then add in minced garlic. Allow to cook another 3–5 minutes.
3. Whisk in flour to make a roux and continue cooking for another minute or so, continuously whisking to prevent burning.
4. Slowly whisk in milk, cream, salt, pepper, and paprika and simmer for about 2–3 minutes.
5. Remove from heat and add in 1½ cups of shredded cheddar cheese. Add more seasoning if needed.
6. Layer ⅓ of potatoes in dish, then pour ⅓ of sauce mixture on top. Repeat this process two more times, ending with cream sauce.
7. Top with remaining ½ cup of shredded cheese and sprinkle the grated Parmesan on top.
8. Cover with aluminum foil and bake for 40 minutes. Remove foil and continue baking for 20–30 minutes until potatoes are tender and top is golden brown.

Nourishing Bone Broth

Yield: *8–10 cups of broth*

Bone broth is a staple in my kitchen, one that I always have on hand. Though store-bought broth will do in a pinch, nothing compares to homemade. For this recipe, I use both chicken and beef bones, but you can just use one or the other. Bone broth is incredibly nourishing and a great way to add extra nutrients to a recipe.

Ingredients

2 pounds beef bones

2 pounds chicken bones (include skin, cartilage, feet . . . everything!)

2 carrots, roughly chopped

1 onion, quartered

2 stalks celery, roughly chopped

1 head garlic, top sliced off to expose garlic cloves

¼ cup apple cider vinegar

1 handful peppercorns

1–2 teaspoons salt

2 bay leaves

1 bundle parsley

1 bundle thyme

8–10 cups water

Instructions

1. Preheat oven to 425°F and lay beef and chicken bones on baking sheet. Roast for 30 minutes, turning halfway through.
2. In a large stock pot, add in bones and all ingredients. Water should cover all ingredients. Add more if needed.
3. Simmer on low for 8–10 hours.
4. Strain liquid and store in mason jars for delicious nourishing bone broth for recipes or just to drink.

Home Fries

Yield: *4–5 servings*

The secret to these homemade French fries is cooking them in coconut oil. I'm not entirely sure why frying in coconut oil is so good, but it is—the fries turn out soft and tender on the inside but firm and crispy on the outside, without leaving a greasy residue on the fries.

Ingredients

3–5 pounds russet potatoes

6 cups unflavored coconut oil (or tallow or lard)

Sea salt to taste

Instructions

1. Wash thoroughly and cut potatoes to fry size. Fill a large bowl with ice water and soak cut potatoes for 15–20 minutes.
2. Once done soaking, remove from water and pat dry.
3. While potatoes are drying, heat oil to 350°F (or test by dropping a fry in; if it bubbles, it's ready).
4. Fry in batches. Grab the first batch of fries and carefully place in oil with tongs or a mesh skimmer. Make sure fries are in one even layer; don't over-crowd the oil.
5. After 5–7 minutes, remove first batch and place on a paper towel-lined baking sheet. The fries won't be crisp and golden and that's okay; they just need to be somewhat tender. Drop the next batch in.
6. After you complete a few batches, start with the original batch and fry once again for another 5–7 minutes, until golden and crispy. This is called double frying. The second fry will finish cooking the potatoes and create the perfect crisp you are looking for.
7. Keep repeating this until all fries have been double fried. Adjust heat as necessary to keep the oil hot enough but not so hot it burns.
8. Sprinkle fries with sea salt and serve fresh and hot.

Homemade Flour Tortillas

Yield: *12 servings*

In my house we have tacos at least once a week, if not more, and if you want to take your next taco night to the next level try these super easy homemade tortillas. In my own tortilla making journey, I learned there is a tad bit of a learning curve to get that perfect size and texture, so don't get discouraged and stick with it—I promise they are worth it in the end.

Ingredients

3 cups all-purpose flour

5 tablespoons cold butter or lard, or
    2 tablespoons bacon fat

1 teaspoon salt

1 cup hot water

Instructions

1. Place flour in a medium-sized mixing bowl.
2. Next, add in butter, lard, or bacon fat. (Using bacon fat gives it some extra flavor and you're not letting it go to waste. Win, win!). Using your hands or a fork, work the fat into the flour and give it a good mix so it's all incorporated.
3. Add in your salt and hot water (I like to slowly add the water, mixing as I go). Mix well with a fork until everything is well incorporated. Place dough on a floured surface and knead for a couple minutes until a smooth ball forms.
4. Place back in bowl, cover, and let rest 1 hour. (This step is optional.)
5. After rise, place dough on a floured work surface and divide the dough into 12 equal portions. Using a tortilla press or rolling pin, roll dough into ¼-inch-thick rounds (about 8-inch circles).
6. Heat skillet (I prefer a cast iron skillet) over medium heat and cook the first tortilla for about 30–45 seconds until little bubbles form on the surface. Then flip over and cook for another 20–30 seconds. Repeat this process with remaining tortillas.
7. Serve warm or save for later in an airtight container.

NOTE

If you want to try grinding your own flour, you can purchase whole wheat berries from a variety of places online. My favorite is Bluebird Farms out of Washington and I use the Nutrimill flour mill/grinder.

Tallow

Yield: *Varies*

I use tallow for so many different things: cooking, skincare, making candles, moisturizer . . . the list could go on and on. But purchasing tallow from the store or online can get expensive very quickly, which is why I started making it at home. It was the best decision. Not only am I saving money, but I can ensure it's high quality and pure. For this recipe, the water and salt measurement is based on filling your slow cooker about half full, up to 1 inch from the top, with the beef fat. The recipe below is for a 7-quart slow cooker.

Ingredients

Pure grass-fed beef fat, any amount (see notes)

2 tablespoons salt

6–8 cups water (if you live in a drier climate, use 8 cups)

TOOLS

Large (7-quart) slow-cooker

Large bowl

Glass jars for storage

Instructions

1. Cut beef fat into 1–2-inch chunks. (I like to place my beef fat in the freezer to harden a bit because it makes it easier to cut.)
2. Place chunks of beef fat in slow-cooker, then add in salt and water and heat on low. As it melts, occasionally stir.
3. Once all of the beef fat has completely melted (how long this process takes will depend on how much fat you are using and how big or small your chunks are), line a metal strainer with a cheesecloth and strain over a large metal bowl.
4. After straining, you should be left with pure liquid. Discard any gristle or chunks that were strained out.
5. Set in a cool place to harden. While tallow is hardening, wash out slow-cooker to prepare to use again.
6. Once hardened, pop out of bowl. You will see brown sediment on the bottom of the tallow cake. Scrape off anything that is brown.
7. Cut into fourths and place back in slow-cooker. Add in more salt and water (same amount as first time) and heat on low until completely melted.
8. Once melted, repeat the same process of straining into a metal bowl and allowing to harden.
9. Once hardened, remove from bowl and scrape off any brown impurities from the tallow cake.

(Continued on next page)

10. At this point, the tallow should be white and pretty pure. If you want, you can keep repeating this process until you have the desired pureness of your tallow. I typically go for 2–3 purifying cycles.
11. Once purified to your liking, I cut the tallow into fourths and place in a metal bowl over a pot of boiling water (double broiler) and melt the tallow once more.
12. Once melted, I carefully ladle into glass jars for storing. As you're ladling, there may still be a little water that separates from the melted tallow (you will see it at the bottom of the bowl). Be careful not to get any water in your storage jars because it will make the tallow spoil.
13. Store in sealed jars at room temperature for up to a few weeks. In fridge or freezer, it will last a very long time.

NOTE

You can reach out to local butchers or ranchers to purchase beef fat. Just be mindful that you are getting it from a quality source. I like to store some tallow for cooking and the rest I whip to create tallow moisturizer for my skull. For face moisturizer, I add in a little jojoba oil for added benefits. The uses for tallow are myriad and includes soaps and candles.

Chicken Turnovers

Yield: *10–12 servings*

> *Until now, this has been a family secret recipe that we make for most parties and holidays, especially Thanksgiving. I can't remember a Thanksgiving where these chicken turnovers weren't made, and they are always the first dish gone.*

Ingredients

DOUGH

1 cup warm milk

½ cup (8 tablespoons) melted butter

1 tablespoon sugar

1 tablespoon instant yeast

2 cups all-purpose flour

1 tablespoon butter for brushing tops

FILLING

2 tablespoons butter

1 medium onion, diced

3–4 cloves garlic, minced

3 pounds chicken tenders

2–3 teaspoons salt

2–3 teaspoons pepper

2–3 teaspoons Italian seasoning

2 (8-ounce) blocks (or 2½ cups) cream cheese

½ cup grated Parmesan

Instructions

1. Start by making the dough. In a small saucepan, warm milk, butter, and sugar until butter is melted. Pour into the mixing bowl of your stand mixer fitted with dough hook. (Mixture should be warm or lukewarm.) If mixing by hand, pour into large mixing bowl. Stir in yeast and wait 1–2 minutes.
2. Slowly add in flour, mixing on low speed until dough forms a soft ball that pulls away from the sides of the bowl. If mixing by hand, place dough on lightly floured surface and knead for 6–8 minutes. Place dough in greased bowl, cover, and let rise 1–2 hours until doubled in size.
3. While dough is rising, make the filling. In a large skillet, melt 2 tablespoons butter over medium heat. Add in diced onion and cook for 2–3 minutes until beginning to soften. Add in garlic and cook 1–2 minutes, then add in chicken tenders and season with salt, pepper, and Italian seasoning. Cook chicken until cooked through, 8–10 minutes. Once cooked, remove chicken from pan and chop.
4. Add chicken back to the pan and add in your cream cheese. Stir until cream cheese is melted, then add in grated Parmesan and stir to incorporate. Remove from heat and allow filling to cool.
5. Preheat oven to 350°F.
6. Once doubled, punch down dough and turn out onto lightly floured surface. Divide into 2 halves and roll out into rectangles that are roughly 9x13 inches. Cut into 10–12 equal-sized squares.
7. The filling should be somewhat cool by now. Fill each square with about 1 tablespoon of filling (don't over-fill or they will be hard to close and seal).
8. Once filled, fold the edges of the dough over the center to form a ball shape. Pinch the seams to seal and place on a large baking sheet lined with parchment paper. Bake for 15 minutes or until golden brown.
9. Repeat process with second half of dough and filling.
10. Once finished baking, brush with a little melted butter, then cool for 5–8 minutes and serve!

The L-7 Twice-Baked Potatoes

Yield: *8 servings*

There is a small-town bar and grill in Idaho called the L-7 Bar & Grill that makes the best twice-baked potatoes. The owner, who is an old friend of mine, was the inspiration for this recipe.

Ingredients

10–12 pieces thick-cut bacon

8 large russet potatoes

2–3 tablespoons olive oil

1½ sticks (¾ cup) butter

1 cup heavy cream

Salt and pepper to taste

1 cup shredded cheese of choice (I like sharp cheddar)

Instructions

1. Cook bacon. I cook my bacon by lining a baking sheet with tin foil, laying bacon down in 1 layer, and placing in the oven on a low broil for about 15 minutes, turning over the bacon halfway through. Once cooked, set aside. Once cool, chop up the bacon into small pieces.
2. Preheat oven to 400°F.
3. Rub each potato with olive oil, place on baking sheet, and bake for 1 hour. Make sure potatoes are fully cooked through.
4. Once cooked, remove potatoes from oven and lower to 350°F.
5. Carefully cut potatoes in half lengthwise and scrape out insides into a large bowl. Place the empty potato skins back on baking sheet.
6. Add butter and cream to potato insides and thoroughly mash to a consistency you like. Add salt and pepper to taste.
7. Scoop the mashed potatoes back into the skins until full, just a little higher than the sides of the skin. I like to think of creating a little hill on top.
8. Top with bacon pieces and a good amount of shredded cheese.
9. Place filled potatoes back in oven and bake for 15–20 minutes until the cheese is melted and a little golden on top.

Stage Coach Baked Beans

Yield: *10 servings*

Growing up around farmers and ranchers, baked beans were a staple, especially during campfire cookouts in the summer. Everyone has their own way of making baked beans and this recipe is a combination of all my favorite elements from the various baked beans I've had over the years.

Ingredients

3 cups dried navy beans (you can substitute with canned navy beans)

10–12 slices bacon, chopped

1 medium onion, diced

1 green bell pepper, seeded and diced

2 cloves garlic, minced

¾ cup plain tomato sauce

1 packed cup brown sugar

2 tablespoons apple cider vinegar

Couple splashes Worcestershire sauce

1 tablespoon yellow mustard

1 teaspoon smoked paprika

2 teaspoons salt

½ teaspoon black pepper

Instructions

1. Place dried beans in a pot and add water until the water is a couple inches higher than the beans. Let soak overnight. Drain beans and bring them to a boil in a pot with fresh water, then simmer for 1 hour. Drain the beans and set aside. Reserve 1½ cups of liquid for later. (If using canned beans, skip this step and just add in step 4.)
2. In a Dutch oven, cook the bacon, then add in diced onion and green peppers, and cook until soft. Add in garlic and cook for a few more minutes.
3. Add in tomato sauce, brown sugar, apple cider vinegar, Worcestershire sauce, yellow mustard, and seasonings. Stir.
4. Pour in beans as well as the reserved liquid you set aside. Simmer for 5–6 minutes.
5. While simmering, preheat oven to 325°F. Cover Dutch oven with lid and place in oven for 30 minutes, until sauce begins to thicken. Remove lid and continue baking for another 30 minutes.

Mama's Famous Roasted Carrots

Yield: *3–4 servings*

The first time my mom made these carrots, I knew I had to get the recipe from her. This carrot recipe is a blend of sweet and savory with the ginger adding the perfect amount of brightness to the flavor. If you want kiddos to eat their veggies, this is a great dish to make.

Ingredients

8–10 large carrots, washed, peeled, and dried

1–2 teaspoons powdered ginger, or 1 tablespoon fresh grated ginger

1 tablespoon brown sugar

1 tablespoon soy sauce

Instructions

1. Preheat oven to 425°F.
2. Place carrots in baking dish and coat evenly with ginger, brown sugar, and soy sauce. Make sure carrots are placed in 1 even layer.
3. Place in oven and bake 20–25 minutes.

Midwest Country Potato Salad

Yield: *8–10 servings*

All regions have different ways of making potato salad, but this is my all-time favorite recipe. I created this by taking the things I love about traditional Midwest potato salad and adding a few things unique to southern potato salad. I could eat this anytime, but I love making this for summer BBQs.

Ingredients

3 pounds (about 8–10) Yukon gold potatoes, peeled and diced into 1-inch cubes

2 cups mayonnaise

2–3 tablespoons yellow mustard

1 tablespoon pickle juice

1 splash apple cider vinegar

1 pinch celery seed

1½ teaspoons sea salt

½ teaspoon black pepper

4 medium-sized pickles, finely chopped

4 hardboiled eggs, peeled and chopped

1 small onion, finely chopped

2 celery stalks, finely chopped

Fresh dill for garnish

Instructions

1. Add cubed potatoes to a large pot, cover with water, and cook until potatoes are fork tender, about 12–15 minutes. Be careful not to overcook potatoes or it will make the potato salad too mushy. Drain potatoes and place on a sheet pan to cool.
2. In a large bowl, whisk together mayonnaise, mustard, pickle juice, apple cider vinegar, celery seed, salt, and pepper.
3. Gently fold in hardboiled egg, potatoes, onion, celery, and pickles until well-combined. Taste and adjust ingredients to your liking.
4. Cover and refrigerate at least 1 hour. I like to make this a day ahead of time—the longer it refrigerates, the more the flavors develop.
5. Garnish with a little fresh chopped dill and serve.

Homemade Chicken Gravy

Yield: *4 servings*

A good homemade chicken gravy is a staple in any kitchen. If I am making mashed potatoes with any type of meat other than beef, I almost always make this chicken gravy recipe. The drippings aren't necessary, but they really add to the flavor.

Ingredients

2 tablespoons butter

3 tablespoons all-purpose flour

2 tablespoons drippings from a roasted chicken (optional, but adds great flavor)

2 cups chicken broth

1 teaspoon onion powder

2 teaspoons garlic powder

½ teaspoon dried thyme

¼ teaspoon dried rosemary

Salt and pepper to taste

Instructions

1. In a saucepan over medium heat, melt butter and whisk in flour to make a roux. Cook for a few minutes continuously (this cooks out the raw flour taste). At this point, if you have drippings, whisk them into the roux.

2. Slowly whisk in chicken broth. Once sauce beings to thicken, lower heat.

3. Add in onion powder, garlic powder, thyme, and rosemary and continue to simmer, whisking frequently to keep from burning. Add in salt and pepper to taste. Simmer for 5–10 minutes until it reaches your desired thickness. If gravy becomes too thick, you can add a splash of broth or heavy cream.

Homemade Beef Gravy

Yield: *4 servings*

I love a good savory beef gravy, especially on top of mashed potatoes paired with a steak, over top my pot roast, or with a large batch of meatballs.

Ingredients

2 tablespoons butter

3 tablespoons all-purpose flour

2 tablespoons drippings from a beef roast (optional, but adds great flavor)

2 cups beef broth

1 teaspoon onion powder

2 teaspoons garlic powder

1 tablespoon Worcestershire sauce

Salt and pepper to taste

Instructions

1. In a saucepan over medium heat, melt butter and whisk in flour to make a roux. Cook for a few minutes, whisking continuously (this cooks out the raw flour taste). At this point, if you have drippings, whisk them into the roux.
2. Slowly whisk in beef broth. Once sauce beings to thicken, lower heat.
3. Add in onion powder, garlic powder, and Worcestershire sauce and continue to simmer, whisking frequently to keep from burning. Add in salt and pepper to taste. Simmer for 5–10 minutes until it reaches your desired thickness. If gravy becomes too thick, you can add a splash of broth.

CHAPTER 6

Snacks

Potato Chips

Yield: *4–6 servings*

In my family we joke that my mom must have eaten a lot of chips when she was pregnant with my sisters and me because we love chips! Even as a kid, I would prefer chips over anything sweet. The wonderful thing about making homemade potato chips is you get all the delicious flavor—more, if you ask me—without all of the yucky ingredients found in most store-bought potato chips.

Ingredients

4–6 Yukon gold potatoes

Oil for frying (I use unflavored coconut oil, but vegetable oil also works)

Sea salt

Instructions

1. Wash potatoes, then, using a mandolin or sharp knife, slice potatoes as thinly as possible (almost paper thin).
2. Fill a bowl with cold water and soak potatoes for at least 20 minutes.
3. Drain water and pat completely dry.
4. In a Dutch oven or other deep pan, heat coconut oil to 350°F, or 400°F if using vegetable oil.
5. Prepare a baking sheet lined with paper towel and set aside for when the potatoes come out of the oil (I like to place a cooling rack on the baking sheet and lay the paper towel on top of that).
6. In small batches, cook the potatoes in the oil, stirring and turning often.
7. Once brown and crispy, remove from oil and place on paper towel. Season with sea salt while still hot.
8. Repeat this process with the remaining potatoes.

Teriyaki Beef Jerky

Yield: *10 servings*

We love beef jerky in our house, but we aren't fans of how much sodium is in traditional store-bought jerky, so we started making our own and, after years of trying different flavor combinations, we finally created a recipe we love and I know you will too.

Ingredients

2 pounds round roast or rump roast

1 packed cup brown sugar

1 cup soy sauce

3 tablespoons fresh-squeezed orange juice

1 teaspoon fresh ground black pepper

1 teaspoon powdered ginger, or 1 tablespoon fresh ginger

Instructions

1. Thinly slice the meat to about ⅛–¼-inch thickness (freezing for 1 hour beforehand makes slicing easier).
2. In a medium-sized bowl, make the marinade by whisking together brown sugar, soy sauce, orange juice, pepper, and ginger.
3. Place meat into marinade and coat evenly. Cover with plastic wrap or transfer to a resealable plastic bag and refrigerate for 12 hours.
4. Line 2 baking sheets with aluminum foil and place a wire rack on top of each.
5. Preheat oven to 175°F with the oven racks in the center of the oven.
6. Place marinated meat in a single layer on the wire racks on baking sheets and place in oven. Bake for 3–4 hours, rotating the pans from top to bottom and front to back halfway through cooking time. When done, meat should be dried through. It should be leather-like in appearance, but still a little tender when you bite into it.
7. Store jerky in airtight container. Jerky will last about a week, but you can refrigerate or freeze for longer.

Homemade Pickles

Yield: *7–9 servings*

One of my favorite memories growing up was our yearly trip to Frankenmuth, MI where we would get fresh barrel pickles from a delicious cheese shop and bakery. I think that is where my love of pickles started. The thing I love most about homemade pickles is that if prepared and fermented correctly, they offer great benefits to your gut health and, of course, they are so delicious. If you want, you can can these pickles and keep them in your pantry for years to come.

Ingredients

6–8 pickling cucumbers

2 cups water

1 cup distilled vinegar

1 tablespoon sea salt

1 teaspoon sugar

Lots of fresh dill (3–4 sprigs per jar)

1 teaspoon mustard seed

6–8 cloves garlic, roughly chopped

1 handful whole peppercorns (I use about 10–12 per jar)

1 pinch red pepper flakes per jar (more if you like a bite)

Instructions

1. Start by cleaning 2 (1-quart) mason jars.
2. Cut your cucumbers into fourths or into ¼-inch thick spears (whichever size you prefer).
3. Make the brine by adding water, vinegar, salt, and sugar to a medium saucepan and bringing to a boil until sugar and salt dissolve. Remove from heat and cool to room temperature.
4. Add the equivalent of about 3 whole cucumbers to each jar. Don't pack too tightly; allow room for the brine. Then add dill, mustard seed, garlic, peppercorns, and red pepper flakes to each jar.
5. Once cooled, add brine to jars, making sure cucumbers are completely covered by brine. Seal tightly with the lid and store in refrigerator for one week, then enjoy! (You can eat them at any time, but the flavor is best after a week.)

NOTE

If you want longer storage than 4–6 weeks, instead of storing in refrigerator you can follow a simple canning method for pickles.

Mild Salsa

Yield: *4 servings*

Living in Arizona, you learn what good authentic salsa is. I love to throw this salsa recipe together for our weekly taco nights. It is so light and refreshing and the perfect side dish or topping on your next taco night.

Ingredients

3 cups peeled and chopped tomatoes (preferably garden-fresh tomatoes)

½ medium onion, chopped

2 jalapeños, chopped, with seeds

2 cloves garlic, chopped

¼–½ cup fresh cilantro

1 pinch cumin

1 pinch sugar

Salt to taste

2 tablespoons lime juice

Instructions

1. Add tomatoes, onion, jalapeños, and garlic to a food processor with cilantro, cumin, sugar, salt, and lime juice.
2. Pulse until desired consistency. I like restaurant-style salsa that is somewhat smooth but still a little chunky, so I typically do 2–4 quick pulses.
3. Place in airtight container and store in fridge. I like to refrigerate mine for at least 2–4 hours before serving.

Homemade Ketchup

Yield: *about 4 cups of prepared ketchup*

I love all ketchup, but nothing beats this homemade recipe. In the recipe, I have included how you would preserve your batch of ketchup by canning. We almost all use ketchup on a regular basis. How nice would it be to just be able to walk to your pantry shelf anytime you need ketchup and not have to worry about going to the store to buy some?

Ingredients

5 pounds tomatoes, chopped

½ onion, chopped

½ clove garlic

½ cup apple cider vinegar

½ cup maple syrup

2 teaspoons salt

¼ teaspoon ground cloves

½ teaspoon mustard seed

½ teaspoon allspice

¼ teaspoon cinnamon

1 pinch cayenne pepper

3–4 half-pint mason jars

Instructions

1. Add tomatoes, onion, and garlic to a pot and bring to a boil until soft, about 30 minutes.
2. Once soft, run though a food mill to remove skins and seeds, then add back to pot with all remaining ingredients. If you don't have a food mill, add in vinegar and hit with an immersion blender, then strain through a fine mesh strainer and add back to pot with all remaining ingredients.
3. Bring to a simmer and cook for 2–3 hours. If you like a thicker ketchup, cook for closer to 3 hours. If you're not canning, allow ketchup to cool, then add to jars, seal with lid, and place in fridge.
4. If you plan on canning, when ketchup is almost at your desired consistency, fill your water bath canner and wash your jars, rings, and lids and place clean jars in canner to stay warm.
5. Once ready, remove jar from your canner and fill your jar with ketchup using a wide mouth funnel until full, leaving ½ inch space from the top (headspace).
6. Insert the back of a spoon or canning wand into the jar a few times to remove any air bubbles, then wipe rim of jar, place lid and ring on, and tighten. Repeat this with all jars, then place into canner. Ensure jars are fully submerged with 1–2 inches of water above the jars.
7. Place lid on canner and bring to a roaring boil. Once at a roaring boil, set timer to 10 minutes.
8. After 10 minutes, turn off heat and remove lid, carefully remove jars from water with canning jar lifter, and place on a towel for 12–24 hours.
9. Remove rings and check to make sure jars sealed properly, then wipe jars clean and store on shelf or in cupboard.

Note: *Improperly canned foods can be dangerous to consume. For more information on proper canning procedures, see the USDA Complete Guide to Home Canning, available online from the National Center for Home Food Preservation.*

Homemade BBQ Sauce

Yield: *about 3 cups*

My husband eats BBQ sauce on just about everything, so this recipe is on repeat in our house. In addition to making it for a condiment, this is also the recipe I use when I'm making BBQ pulled chicken or pork, BBQ chicken pizza, topping my meatloaf, and a myriad of other dishes.

Ingredients

2 cups ketchup (homemade, page 150, or store-bought)

1 cup brown sugar

2 tablespoons apple cider vinegar

3 teaspoons Worcestershire sauce

3 teaspoons chili powder

2 teaspoons salt

2 teaspoons garlic powder

2 teaspoons paprika

1 pinch black pepper

Instructions

1. In medium saucepan, whisk together all ingredients and bring to a simmer. Simmer for 30–35 minutes, until all sugar is dissolved and sauce has thickened.
2. Remove from heat, ladle into jars, and allow to cool completely. Add lid and store in refrigerator.

Homemade PB Granola

Yield: *5 cups*

One of my favorite breakfasts is what I call PB&J yogurt. I love to load my yogurt bowl up with this PB granola and add in some sliced strawberries, a tablespoon or so of peanut butter, and a drizzle of local honey.

Ingredients

3 cups rolled oats

1 cup slivered almonds

1 cup sunflower seeds

1 pinch cinnamon

1 pinch sea salt

½ cup peanut butter

⅓ cup maple syrup

1 teaspoon vanilla

¼ cup coconut oil

Instructions

1. Preheat oven to 350°F and line a baking sheet with parchment paper.
2. In a large bowl, mix together oats, almonds, sunflower seeds, cinnamon, and salt. Set aside.
3. In a small saucepan, melt peanut butter, maple syrup, vanilla, and coconut oil while stirring continuously.
4. Once melted, pour over oat mixture and stir until combined.
5. Spread granola mixture across baking sheet in an even layer and place in oven.
6. Bake for 30 minutes, stirring halfway through.
7. Remove from oven and cool. Once completely cooled, break into pieces and store in airtight container.

Homemade Peanut Butter Chocolate Granola Bars

Yield: *12 servings*

Granola bars are a great easy snack for around the house or when you're on the go, or even if you are craving something sweet but want something fairly healthy.

Ingredients

3 cups rolled oats

1 cup slivered almonds

1 cup sunflower seeds

1 pinch cinnamon

1 pinch sea salt

½ cup peanut butter

⅓ cup maple syrup

1 teaspoon vanilla

½ cup chocolate chips

1 tablespoon coconut oil

Instructions

1. In a large bowl, mix together oats, almonds, sunflower seeds, cinnamon, and salt. Set aside.
2. In a small saucepan, melt peanut butter, maple syrup, and vanilla while continuously stirring.
3. Once melted, pour over oat mixture and stir until combined.
4. Line a 9 × 13-inch baking dish with parchment paper, allowing the parchment paper to come up the sides of the dish.
5. Add in the granola and press into a thick flat layer. Put in refrigerator for 15 minutes.
6. Either in microwave or small saucepan, melt together chocolate chips and coconut oil.
7. Remove granola from refrigerator and drizzle melted chocolate on top. Cover with plastic wrap and place back in refrigerator overnight.
8. After they have chilled, you can either leave them in the baking dish or remove and cut into 2-inch-thick bars and store in airtight container. I like to keep them in the refrigerator for storage.

Homemade Applesauce

Yield: *6 servings*

Growing up in the Midwest, every fall we would go to a local orchard, take a hay ride through the apple trees, load our baskets up with fresh apples, then go back to the barn where they would make fresh homemade applesauce with the apples you picked. It was the most delicious applesauce I had ever tasted, and I wanted to create a recipe that could bring that experience into your kitchen. This is also a recipe you can multiply and make large batches of and water bath can for food storage.

Ingredients

6 pounds apples peeled, cored, and cut into chunks

1–2 tablespoons maple syrup (if you want a sweeter applesauce)

2 teaspoons cinnamon

½ cup water

1 tablespoon lemon juice

Instructions

1. In a Dutch oven or large pot, add your apples, maple syrup, cinnamon, and water. Cover and simmer on medium heat for 15–20 minutes (apples should be tender).
2. Add to a food processor or use an immersion blender and blend to desired consistency. Stir in lemon juice and adjust taste as necessary, adding more cinnamon, maple syrup, or lemon juice to achieve your desired taste. I like my applesauce heavy on the cinnamon.
3. Transfer to a large jar and, once cooled, seal with lid and store in refrigerator.

Sourdough Soft Pretzels

Yield: *12 servings*

Any time we go out to a restaurant that has soft Bavarian-style pretzels, we always order one. They never disappoint and are such a great little snack, so I decided to learn how to make my own sourdough version and let me tell you, they are so delicious! I have included cup measurements in the directions but if possible I strongly recommend weighing your ingredients on a food scale because it can alter the outcome of the pretzels.

Note: *I typically make the dough the night before and let it rest overnight.*

Ingredients

105 grams (½ cup) active sourdough starter

505 grams (4¼ cups) bread four

260 grams (1 cup) filtered water

15 grams (2½ teaspoons) sea salt

45 grams (1 tablespoon) honey

2 tablespoons baking soda

1 tablespoon brown sugar

1–2 tablespoons coarse sea salt (or pretzel salt)

1 egg, beaten

Instructions

1. Six to twelve hours before making the pretzel dough, feed your starter (see page 3 for feeding instructions).
2. Place all ingredients except baking soda and brown sugar in the bowl of your stand mixer fitted with the dough hook. Mix on lowest speed for 6–8 minutes. If you do not have a stand mixer, knead by hand for 10–12 minutes).
3. Cover bowl and let rest for 10–12 hours (see notes).
4. Turn dough out onto a clean surface and divide into 12 equal portions. Shape each piece of dough into pretzel shape and place on baking sheet lined with parchment paper.
5. Cover with towel and let sit for 30–60 minutes or until puffy.
6. Bring 6 cups of water to boil. Add baking soda and brown sugar.
7. Preheat oven to 425°F. Place rack in center of oven.
8. Boil each pretzel for 1 minute (30 seconds on each side). Return pretzels to baking sheet.
9. Brush each pretzel with beaten egg and sprinkle with salt.
10. Bake 12–14 minutes or until golden brown on the outside.

Brooks Family Hummus

Yield: *12–14 servings*

My husband's family is Lebanese and his mom, Zizi, makes the most incredible authentic hummus and I knew that I had to share her recipe with you. It also seems too good to be true how simple this hummus recipe is, but trust me, it's divine. Store-bought hummus does not even begin to compare to this recipe.

Ingredients

6 cloves fresh garlic, peeled

2 (15-ounce) cans garbanzo beans (chickpeas)

¼ cup tahini

1 tablespoon salt

1 tablespoon lemon juice

Instructions

1. Place garlic in food processor and pulse until minced.
2. Add in garbanzo beans and tahini and blend until smooth.
3. Add in lemon juice and salt and continue blending until desired consistency.
4. Adjust taste to your desired preference.

NOTE

Feel free to season with salt, lemon juice, and garlic—add or subtract based on your taste preference. I recommend using fresh garlic cloves, but garlic powder or pre-minced garlic would work just fine too. Our preferred brand of tahini is Mid-East, but any brand would work.

Healthy Grape Gummies

Yield: *8 servings*

Sometimes it's nice to have a cool, refreshing treat, especially in the summer, that is not loaded with processed sugar. This recipe calls for grape juice, but you could use any flavor of juice you like—grape just happens to be my favorite. I have also made these with strawberry-mango juice and they were delicious as well. Have fun with the recipe and get creative.

Ingredients

3 cups grape juice (I use Lakewood Organic, not from concentrate)

1 cup pure coconut water

6 tablespoons grass-fed gelatin (I use Perfect Supplements brand)

Sweetener of choice, optional

Instructions

1. In a medium pot, pour in grape juice and coconut water, then sprinkle gelatin on top and let sit to allow the gelatin to bloom.
2. After gelatin has bloomed, heat over low heat just until the mixture melts. If you want to add a sweetener of choice, this is when you would add it. You could add maple syrup, honey, sugar, or whatever you would like. I leave a sweetener out, but that's my preference.
3. Pour into a glass dish. I use an 8 × 10-inch glass dish. You can also use any shaped silicon mold.
4. Place in refrigerator. After about 24 hours or once the gummies set, enjoy!

Healthy Fruit Leather

Yield: *10–12 servings*

Who didn't love Fruit Roll-Ups as a kid? I know I did, but now that I understand different ingredients and how they affect our bodies, most fruit roll-ups are not something I would choose to eat. That's why I wanted to learn how to make fruit leather. Fruit leather is basically a healthier (more delicious, in my opinion) version of a fruit roll-up.

Ingredients

4 cups fresh fruit (strawberries, peaches, apricots, mixed berries, etc.)

½ cup water

Lemon juice to taste

Sweetener of choice, optional

Instructions

1. After washing and prepping your fruit, add to pot with water and bring to a simmer. Cover and let cook on low for about 15 minutes. (If you are making a larger batch, my rule of thumb is ½ cup water for every 4 cups of fruit).
2. Add in lemon juice, 1 teaspoon at a time, to achieve your desired taste; the lemon juice is just to brighten the flavor. I typically do 1–2 teaspoons of lemon juice for 4 cups of fruit.
3. If you choose to add in any sugar or other sweetener, add it now, adding small amounts at a time until you reach your desired sweetness.
4. Cook for another 8–10 minutes until purée starts to thicken.
5. Pour the purée into a food processor, blender, or use an immersion blender to blend the purée until very smooth.
6. If you have a dehydrator, pour the puree on trays and dehydrate as directed. If you do not have a dehydrator, preheat oven to 140°F or as low as your oven will go. Pour your fruit purée onto a baking sheet lined with parchment paper. Place in oven and bake for 4–6 hours or until no longer tacky.
7. Remove from oven and cool completely.
8. Once cooled, cut into 2-inch strips (if you cut the parchment paper along with the leather, it acts as the wrapper) and roll up. Store in container or resealable plastic bag and enjoy!

Guacamole

Yield: *4–5 servings*

I'm a little embarrassed to admit that I had never tried guacamole until I was in my twenties because I just thought it looked gross. I was a picky eater back in the day. But boy was I missing out. For a long time after I tried and enjoyed guacamole, I would buy it from the store, but it never tasted as good as fresh-made from the Mexican restaurants in Arizona, so I started making my own. It's delicious and only takes a few minutes.

Ingredients

4–6 ripe avocados

½ red onion, finely chopped

1 seeded and finely chopped jalapeño

1 handful chopped cilantro

Garlic powder to taste

Lime or lemon juice to taste

Sea salt to taste

Instructions

1. Slice avocados in half, remove pits, and scoop out the insides into a medium-sized bowl. Mash with a fork.
2. Mix in chopped onion, jalapeño, and cilantro. Continue mashing to the consistency you like.
3. Mix in garlic, lemon, or lime juice and sea salt to taste.
4. Store in refrigerator. To keep it from turning brown, cover with plastic wrap pressed all of the way down to the guacamole so there is no air, then cover top with tin foil.

Mayonnaise

Yield: *about 2 cups*

I started making mayonnaise at home because I was not a fan of the inflammatory seed oils commonly used in most store-bought mayonnaises, and what I realized is mayonnaise is one of the easiest things you can make. It uses minimal ingredients you probably already have on hand and it only takes a few minutes to whip up.

Ingredients

1 cup olive oil or avocado oil

2 large egg yolks at room temperature

1 teaspoon Dijon mustard

3 teaspoons lemon juice

Salt and pepper to taste

Instructions

In a food processor, blender, or a jar (with an immersion blender), whip together all ingredients until well combined and the texture of traditional mayonnaise.

NOTE

Feel free to adjust the amount of mustard, lemon juice, and salt and pepper to your liking. Everyone has their own idea of how mayonnaise should taste.

CHAPTER 7

Quick Breads and Sweets

My Famous Chocolate Chip Cookies

Yield: *18–20 cookies*

A part of me can't believe I am sharing this recipe with the world; this recipe is my baby. It is by far the most sought-after recipe of mine amongst my friends and family. I have spent years tweaking and perfecting these chocolate chip cookies and I can't wait for them to become famous to your friends and family, too.

Ingredients

3 cups all-purpose flour

1½ teaspoons baking soda

2 teaspoons sea salt, divided

1 cup (2 sticks) butter (room temperature or slightly colder)

½ cup white sugar

1½ cups brown sugar

2 eggs + 1 egg yolk

4 teaspoons alcohol-free vanilla extract (regular vanilla extract will work, but try the alcohol-free vanilla—trust me!)

1–2 cups chocolate chips

Instructions

1. Place rack in center of oven and preheat oven to 375°F. Line baking sheet with parchment paper.
2. In a medium bowl, whisk together flour, baking soda, and 1 teaspoon salt. Set aside.
3. In a stand mixer fitted with paddle attachment (or in a large bowl with hand mixer), cream together the butter, white sugar, and brown sugar until smooth and fluffy (6–8 minutes).
4. Add in eggs and egg yolk and beat until blended. Add in vanilla and remaining 1 teaspoon salt. Cream together for another 5 minutes.
5. Turn off mixer and pour the flour mixture into the bowl. Mix on low speed until just combined.
6. Fold in chocolate chips with a spoon or spatula.
7. Drop large spoonfuls onto baking sheet (do not flatten the dough).
8. Place baking sheet of cookie dough balls into the fridge for at least 30 minutes. You could even cover and refrigerate overnight to let the flavors develop.
9. Bake for 8 minutes. Remove from oven and let cool for 3–5 minutes, then transfer to wire cooling rack.
10. Store in airtight container.

Sourdough Pumpkin Muffins

Yield: *about 16 muffins*

These pumpkin muffins made with sourdough starter are heavenly. Using the starter in the muffin batter creates a rich flavor and makes the muffins so moist and fluffy. This is, by far, my family's favorite fall baked good. I love to eat one of these muffins in the morning while drinking a nice cup of hot coffee—probably not the most nutritious breakfast, but it sure makes the soul feel good.

Ingredients

180 grams (1¼ cups) all-purpose flour

1 teaspoon baking soda

1 teaspoon baking powder

½ teaspoon sea salt

2 tablespoons cinnamon

1 teaspoon pumpkin pie spice

2 eggs

½ cup brown sugar

1 cup pumpkin purée

½ cup melted butter

½ cup milk

250 grams (1 cup) active sourdough starter

1 teaspoon vanilla extract

Instructions

1. Place rack in center of oven and preheat to 425°F. Place baking cups in muffin baking pan.
2. In a medium bowl, whisk together flour, baking soda, baking powder, salt, cinnamon, and pumpkin pie spice and set aside.
3. In a medium bowl whisk together eggs and brown sugar until well combined.
4. Whisk into the egg and sugar mixture the pumpkin purée, butter, milk, active sourdough starter, and vanilla.
5. Pour dry ingredients into wet ingredients and stir until just combined (don't over-mix).
6. Spoon batter into muffin tins, filling each cup almost to the top.
7. Bake muffins for 5 minutes. Lower oven temperature to 350°F and continue baking for 10 minutes or until toothpick inserted in the center comes out clean.
8. Let cool 8–10 minutes, then transfer to wire rack to finish cooling.

Banana Bread

Yield: *1 loaf*

The secret of this banana bread is making the banana concentrate, which really enhances the banana flavor. And if you want to switch things up, this loaf is delicious with chocolate chips mixed in.

Ingredients

5–6 large bananas

3 cups all-purpose flour

2 teaspoons baking soda

2 teaspoons baking powder

1 teaspoon salt

½ cup (1 stick) melted butter

1 cup light brown sugar

2 eggs

3 teaspoons vanilla

1 tablespoon cinnamon

¼ teaspoon nutmeg

½ cup chopped walnuts

2 tablespoons sugar for topping

Instructions

1. Place rack in center of oven and preheat to 450°F. Grease 9 × 13-inch loaf pan.
2. Peel and place bananas in microwave-safe bowl, cover with plastic wrap, and microwave for 5 minutes.
3. While bananas microwave, measure out flour, baking soda, baking powder, and salt. Whisk together in a medium bowl and set aside.
4. Carefully remove bananas from microwave and scoop into a fine mesh strainer over a bowl. Let liquid from bananas drain for about 15 minutes, then pour into a small saucepan and bring to a boil. Boil 10–15 minutes until liquid reduces to half of the volume. In another small pan or in microwave, melt butter.
5. Pour butter and brown sugar in bowl with banana liquid and whisk together. Add in eggs, vanilla, cinnamon, and nutmeg and whisk until combined. Add mashed bananas to mixture and combine.
6. Fold flour mixture into wet mixture and stir until combined (don't over-mix). Fold in chopped walnuts. Pour batter into greased pan and bake for 55–65 minutes. Halfway through, remove from oven, sprinkle sugar on top, then continue baking for the remaining time.

Zucchini Bread

Yield: *1 loaf*

I am a bread fanatic, and zucchini bread is no exception. This is such a flavorful recipe and, served warm with nice pat of fresh butter, you just can't beat it. I love enjoying this treat with my morning coffee.

Ingredients

5 large zucchinis

3 cups all-purpose flour

2 teaspoons baking soda

2 teaspoons baking powder

1 teaspoon salt

½ cup (1 stick) melted butter

1 cup light brown sugar

3 eggs

3 teaspoons vanilla

1 tablespoon cinnamon

¼ teaspoon nutmeg

½ cup chopped walnuts

2 tablespoons sugar for topping

Instructions

1. Place oven rack in center of oven and preheat to 450°F. Grease a 9 × 13-inch loaf pan.
2. Grate zucchini, then, using a cheesecloth, wring out as much liquid as you can.
3. In a medium-sized bowl, whisk together flour, baking soda, baking powder, and salt and set aside.
4. Pour butter and brown sugar in bowl and whisk together. Add in eggs, vanilla, cinnamon, and nutmeg and whisk until combined. Add grated zucchini to mixture and combine.
5. Fold in flour mixture and stir until combined (don't over-mix). Fold in chopped walnuts. Pour batter into greased pan and bake for 55–65 minutes. Halfway through, remove from oven, sprinkle sugar on top then continue baking for the remaining time.

Nourishing Hot Cocoa

Yield: *2 servings*

Nothing warms up your soul like a hot cup of cocoa, but it's not necessarily the most nutritious drink of choice . . . until now. Bone broth is full of nutrients and by adding it to the hot cocoa you are getting that favorite sweet treat while nourishing yourself.

Ingredients

2 cups beef bone broth

1 cup milk of choice (I prefer raw milk)

2 tablespoons unsweetened cocoa

1 tablespoon sugar of choice

1 tablespoon pure maple syrup (*or substitute for 1 tablespoon sugar of choice*)

1 teaspoon vanilla

1 pinch salt

1 pinch of cinnamon

Marshmallows (page 180), optional

Whipped cream (page 35), optional

Instructions

1. Pour all ingredients into medium saucepan and heat on low-medium heat. Heat all ingredients, stirring occasionally, until hot, just before boiling. (Be careful to not over-heat and burn cocoa).

2. Serve with marshmallows, whipped cream, or any toppings you like!

Homemade Maple Vanilla Marshmallows

Yield: *12 servings*

Store-bought marshmallows have always had a very unnatural taste to me, which is why I love this recipe. These marshmallows are soft, pillowy clouds of sweet goodness. They are great in rice crispy treats, hot cocoa, and of course, s'mores.

Ingredients

2 tablespoons arrowroot powder or powdered sugar

1 cup water, divided

3 tablespoons bovine gelatin (Perfect Supplements is my favorite brand)

1 cup maple syrup

2 teaspoons vanilla

Instructions

1. Line an 8 × 8-inch dish with parchment paper and sprinkle with arrowroot powder or powdered sugar (this prevents sticking).
2. In a mixing bowl, add in ½ cup water and sprinkle gelatin on top to bloom (do not mix in). Let sit for 8–10 minutes.
3. In a saucepan, whisk remaining water, maple syrup, and vanilla and bring to boil. Heat until it reaches 240°F or about 10 minutes.
4. Pour heated mixture into bloomed gelatin while whisking on low. Then whisk on medium speed for 4–5 minutes until soft peaks form.
5. Pour into lined dish and spread out evenly. Place in fridge for 4–6 hours until firm.
6. Once firm, remove from fridge and cut into squares with a greased knife. Toss the squares in a little arrowroot powder or powdered sugar. Store in fridge.

Krystal's Famous Cheesecake

Yield: *8 servings*

As much as I would love to take credit for this cheesecake recipe, I cannot. My sister Krystal is an amazing baker and this recipe is all hers. It is so good I knew I had to add it to the book.

Ingredients

3 sleeves graham crackers

3 tablespoons butter, melted

3 (8-ounce) packages cream cheese

1 cup sugar

3 tablespoons all-purpose flour

1 cup sour cream

1 tablespoon + 1 teaspoon vanilla extract

4 large eggs (room temperature)

Instructions

1. Pre-heat oven to 350°F.
2. In a food processor, blend graham crackers until fine with no clumps. Mix in melted butter.
3. Press into a 9-inch springform pan with about 1½ inches up the side of the pan.
4. Bake for 10–12 minutes, then place in freezer to cool.
5. Lower oven to 300°F.
6. Remove pan from freezer and tightly wrap outside in tin foil so no water can get into pan.
7. In a large bowl, mix together cream cheese, sugar, and flour until well combined. Whether you are using an electric hand mixer or stand mixer, use a low speed to keep too much air from getting in.
8. Add in sour cream and vanilla. Mix on low speed.
9. Slowly mix in 1 egg at a time, scraping down the sides in between eggs.
10. Pour cheesecake batter into pan.
11. Place the springform pan in a larger pan, such as a roasting pan.
12. Fill roasting pan with enough water to reach halfway up the cake pan.
13. Bake for 1 hour.
14. After 1 hour, turn oven off and leave cheesecake in oven for another 30 minutes. (DO NOT open door as it will release the heat; just turn off oven.)
15. Crack open oven door and leave in oven for another 30 minutes. This method of cooling helps prevents the cheesecake from cracking.
16. Remove cheesecake from oven and chill 5–6 hours.

Rustic Layer Cake

Yield: *10–12 servings*

Over the last five years or so, rustic layer cakes have gained a lot of popularity. I personally like them because they are simple to make and don't need a lot of frosting, which is a plus for me because I'm not a fan of frosting. Feel free to get creative and play with your fruit selection and layer fillings.

Ingredients

3 cups cake flour

1 teaspoon salt

1 tablespoon baking powder

½ cup (1 stick) butter, softened

½ cup olive oil

1½ cups sugar

3 eggs + 1 egg white

3 tablespoons vanilla

1 cup milk

2 cups thinly sliced strawberries or berry of choice

Cream Cheese Frosting (page 187)

Instructions

1. Preheat oven to 325°F. Grease 2 (9-inch) cake pans and line bottoms with parchment paper (cut paper into circles to fit the bottom).
2. In a separate bowl, sift together flour, salt, and baking powder. Set aside.
3. In a large bowl, whisk together butter and olive oil for 3–5 minutes.
4. Slowly add in sugar and whisk on high until light and fluffy.
5. Whisk in eggs and egg white one at a time.
6. Whisk in vanilla.
7. Add in milk and keep whisking on high for a few more minutes to make cake batter airy and fluffy.
8. Slowly whisk in flour mixture ¼ at a time.
9. Divide the cake batter evenly between the two cake pans. Bake for 30 minutes or until a toothpick inserted into the center of the cakes comes out clean.
10. Remove from oven and transfer to cooling rack. Once completely cooled, cut the two cake rounds in half to make four cake layers. Place first layer on a large plate or cake stand. Frost the first layer with Cream Cheese Frosting. Add a thin layer of strawberry slices, place the second layer on top, and repeat.
11. Repeat with third layer, then lay fourth cake layer on top. Frost with Cream Cheese Frosting and decorate with fresh berries.

Cream Cheese Frosting

Yield: *about 3 cups*

I often find that frosting is too sweet and too heavy for my taste, but this recipe changes the game. The orange juice really brightens up the flavor while balancing the sweetness of the powdered sugar.

Ingredients

½ cup (1 stick) unsalted butter, softened

8 ounces cream cheese

1 teaspoon vanilla extract

1 cup heavy whipping cream

1 pound powdered sugar

½–1 teaspoon fresh-squeezed orange juice

Sea salt, optional

Instructions

1. In a medium bowl, whisk together softened butter and cream cheese by hand or using an electric mixer.
2. Mix in vanilla.
3. In a separate bowl, whip 1 cup heavy cream until soft peaks form. Fold into cream cheese and butter mixture.
4. Slowly add in powdered sugar, 1 cup at a time, scraping down sides in between cups until you reach your desired sweetness and consistency. (I typically use ¾ of a 1-pound bag of powdered sugar.
5. Whisk in orange juice.
6. Store in an airtight container.

NOTE

If you find the frosting too sweet, add in sea salt ⅛ teaspoon at a time until you reach your desired sweetness.

Double Chocolate Fudge Brownies

Yield: *9 servings*

Brownies are a tried-and-true sweet treat in any kitchen. These brownies are soft and chewy in the center with the perfect crunch on the outside and sweet little surprises throughout from the chocolate chips. My favorite way to serve them is warm with a big scoop of vanilla ice cream.

Ingredients

¾ cup (1½ sticks) butter

1½ cups brown sugar, packed

2 eggs, room temperature

1 cup unsweetened cocoa powder

2 teaspoons vanilla

½ teaspoon salt

6 tablespoons all-purpose flour

½ cup semi-sweet chocolate chips

Instructions

1. Preheat oven to 350°F. Grease and line an 8 × 8-inch baking pan with parchment paper.
2. In a medium saucepan, whisk together butter and sugar over low-medium heat until the mixture is melted and glossy.
3. Remove from heat and pour into a large mixing bowl.
4. Allow to cool slightly and then whisk in 1 egg at a time.
5. Whisk in cocoa powder, vanilla, and salt.
6. Gently fold in flour, then chocolate chips.
7. Pour into baking pan and bake for 25–30 minutes. Insert a toothpick into center to check for doneness. When the toothpick comes out with just a little batter on it but edges of brownies are firm, you know it's done.

Caramel Dutch Apple Pie

Yield: *8 servings*

What is more American than apple pie? Caramel Dutch Apple Pie with homemade caramel sauce. Well, maybe it doesn't sound more American, but it is out of this world delicious, especially when you top it with homemade vanilla ice cream. I make one every Thanksgiving and Christmas and there is never a single crumb left in the pie pan.

Ingredients

SWEET PIE CRUST

1½ cups all-purpose flour

½ teaspoon salt

½ cup (1 stick) butter

2 tablespoons sugar

¼ cup ice cold water

FILLING

3–4 honey crisp apples, peeled, cored, and thinly sliced

3–4 granny Smith apples, peeled, cored, and thinly sliced

1 tablespoon all-purpose flour

¼ cup brown sugar

1 cup granulated sugar

2 teaspoons cinnamon

¼ teaspoon nutmeg

1 tablespoon lemon juice

CARAMEL SAUCE

1 cup packed brown sugar

6 tablespoons room temperature butter

½ cup heavy cream

1 pinch salt

Instructions

1. Prepare the Sweet Pie Crust to allow to chill in fridge. In a medium bowl, add flour and salt. Cut butter in cubes and add to bowl. Cut butter in with a pastry cutter or fork until the mixture is crumbly and butter is pea-sized. Mix in sugar.

2. Add in ice water 1 tablespoon at a time, mixing in with a fork. You may not need all of the water and be careful not to over-mix. Once combined, mold into a ball and gently press the dough with your hand to flatten into a disc shape. Wrap in plastic wrap and place in fridge while you prepare the Filling.

3. To prepare the Filling, add apple slices to a large bowl and mix in flour, brown sugar, sugar, cinnamon, nutmeg, and lemon juice. Set aside while you make the caramel sauce.

4. To make the Caramel Sauce, in a medium-sized saucepan, heat brown sugar on medium-low heat, stirring every 20–30 seconds. The sugar will form clumps at first, then start to melt.

5. Once sugar is completely melted (keep a close eye on it as it will burn quickly), remove from heat and stir in butter. Be prepared, it will bubble a lot.

6. Keep stirring and add in cream and salt. Keep stirring until everything is combined and you have a smooth, creamy caramel sauce.

7. Transfer to a small bowl or jar to cool a little.

8. Remove pie crust from fridge and turn out onto a lightly floured surface.

(Continued on next page)

(Continued on next page)

STREUSEL TOPPING

1 cup all-purpose flour

½ cup (1 stick) butter

¼ cup granulated sugar

½ cup brown sugar

1 teaspoon cinnamon

9. Roll out into roughly a 9-inch circle, starting from the center and working out in all directions.
10. Preheat oven to 375°F and place pie crust in bottom of pie pan. Cut off any extra crust that hangs over the edge.
11. Take your caramel sauce and pour into the apple filling mixture, giving it a good stir, and pour that into the pie pan lined with the crust. Now make the Streusel Topping.
12. In a small bowl with a fork, mix together flour, butter, sugar, brown sugar, and cinnamon. Topping should be a crumbly texture.
13. Top with the streusel and bake for 50–55 minutes.

Measurement Conversions

Active Dried Yeast Conversion to Sourdough Starter

1 package of yeast (7 grams) = 1 cup of active sourdough starter
For every 1 cup of sourdough starter used, reduce flour and liquid by ½ cup each.

1 cup = 16 tablespoons = 48 teaspoons

¾ cup = 12 tablespoons = 36 teaspoons

⅔ cup = 10 tablespoons + 2 teaspoon = 32 teaspoons

½ cup = 8 tablespoons = 24 teaspoons

⅓ cup 5 tablespoons + 1 teaspoons = 16 teaspoons

¼ cup = 4 tablespoons = 12 teaspoons

⅛ cup = 2 tablespoons = 6 teaspoons

¹⁄₁₆ cup = 1 tablespoon = 3 teaspoon

Oven Temperatures

Fahrenheit	Celsius	Gas Mark
225°	110°	¼
250°	120°	½
275°	140°	1
300°	150°	2
325°	160°	3
350°	180°	4
375°	190°	5
400°	200°	6
425°	220°	7
450°	230°	8

Index